𝕵ustly 𝕻roud

A GERMAN AMERICAN FAMILY
IN INDIANA

Beverly Raffensperger Fauvre

Guild Press of Indiana

All rights reserved under International and Pan-American Copyright
Conventions. Published in the United States by

Guild Press of Indiana, Inc.
6000 Sunset Lane
Indianapolis, IN 46208

Library of Congress Number 95-77937

ISBN: 1-878208-61-6

Manufactured in the United States of America.

About the Cover:

The cover design is a rendering of the architect's plan for the Athenaeum, a watercolor done by W. Campbell in 1896, and graciously loaned for this publication by the Athenaeum Foundation, Inc.

The Athenaeum Foundation is a nonprofit 503C Corporation located at 401 East Michigan Street, Indianapolis, Indiana. The Foundation accepts gifts for the renovation of its historic building, and its ongoing affairs.

Dedication

This book is dedicated to David Van Allen Fauvre, my life
partner, a most loving husband and father, a kind and
incredibly generous man, who has stood by me and my family since
the time when he was not yet a grown man.

And to our children, David William and Cynthia Elise,
who are already carrying on the best of the traditions.

Thanks to the organizations who are dedicated to researching the Indiana German Heritage. They include

University Library and Ruth Lilly Archives and Special Collections, Indiana University-Purdue University, Indianapolis

Max Kade German American Center, IUPUI

Indiana German Heritage Society, Inc.

Deutsche Haus-Athenaeum
401 East Michigan Street
Indianapolis, IN 46204

Contents

Foreword

As the only child and only grandchild in my Bauer-Raffensperger family, I inherited all of the saved letters, stories, scrapbooks, news-clippings and photo albums spanning a period of over a hundred and forty years. I treasured this inheritance and planned to one day use this material to research and write a family history for my children, the only descendents of this German American family. Once I began the project, I found myself in awe of the legacy left to me by five generations.

In researching and studying the lives of my ancestors I came to more fully appreciate their contributions to the growth of Indianapolis and began to feel that they had entrusted me with the task of sharing their stories and creativity with both family and others of German American descent, particularly in Indiana.

While completing this family history, celebrated cousin Kurt Vonnegut, Jr. shared his personal comments and remembrances with me. I am particularly grateful and have included them in the book.

Besides my own personal material, library research, and interviews, my primary source for the history of German Americans in Indianapolis was the book *The Germans in Indianapolis, 1840-1918* by George Theodore Probst. I used the revised and illustrated edition by Eberhard Reichmann, which was published in 1989 by the German American Center and Indiana German Heritage Society, Inc. To help tell the story of my father's association with the Indianapolis Water Co. I referred to and quoted from *Water Runs Downhill* by Marjie Gates Giffin, privately published in 1981. I have made every effort to be accurate in this history of one German American family in Indianapolis, but I know that errors in memory are inevitable and that anyone familiar with my family might tell the story a little differently than I have.

Beverly Raffensperger Fauvre
La Quinta, California 1995

Acknowledgments

As my grandmother and great grandmother did, I have always enjoyed writing. To have the opportunity to work with professionals on a subject so dear to me has been a dream come true. I want to first thank Nancy Niblack Baxter of Guild Press for her immediate interest in my original manuscript and for encouraging me to accept the challenge of reworking it with her help for publication. I also owe a special debt of gratitude to my friend Anne McFarlane Sorden of Saratoga, California for casually mentioning one day that she had once been a professional editor and would edit my family history! Little did she know at the time that her work would help me interest a publisher. Though living in different parts of California most of the year, we worked together over the phone and more often via e-mail with attached files. A perfectionist, Anne has been the best English teacher I've had since Miss McCullough at Tudor Hall School. Under the guidance and direction of Nancy Baxter we saw the book through several incarnations. Anne's indomitable sense of humor kept my spirits up through the frustrating job of revision after revision.

I would also like to acknowledge the following people for their encouragement and help: Andrew G. Burke, an artistic friend and soon to be son-in-law who designed and illustrated the genealogy; David V. Burns, retired architect and past president of the Indiana Historical Society, who shared his memories of his old friends Ed and Bill and the Raffensperger family. Joellen Castetter, Senior Vice President of Raffensperger, Hughes & Co. has written an excellent history of the fifty-seven year old investment banking firm and I was glad to have access to that history. Al Gisler, Jr., the last president of Ko-We-Ba Foods shared his memories, time and knowledge of the company cofounded by my great-grandfather. Mary Fauvre Holmes, my husband's cousin, introduced me to the *Essays* of her great-uncle, John G. Rauch. Giles R. Hoyt, Associate Dean of the Office of International Affairs, IUPUI, reintroduced me to the Atheneaum and introduced me to the German-American Center and the German-American Archives. The papers and letters once belonging to Philip Sachs are now in the archives at IUPUI. Marianne Hughes, the widow of Shannon Hughes, shared her memories and offered encouragement. Elizabeth Davenport Humston and her daughter Janet Humston who share a common Branham ancestry wrote me of their memories of the Branham, Bauer and Raffensperger families and shared their collection of family photographs.

Shubrick Kothe, a nephew of William Kothe, co-founder of Ko-We-Ba, was willing to be interviewed for this history. He provided insight into the lives of German American families in Indianapolis like the Kothes and the Bauers. Marcia Wheeler Mussman suggested I contact her friend Nancy Baxter of Guild Press. Her husband, my cousin, Richard A. Mussman, clarified our common Shockley family history and entertained me with the history of his father, Papa Dick Mussman. Doris Alexander Ochiltree, sister of Alberta Alexander Raffensperger, shared her memories of the Raffensperger family. John G. Rauch, Jr., attorney, shared his memories of my parents. Byron Rutledge, D.D.S., shared his remembrances of the Shockley family and his cousin, my mother. I want to thank Martha Wright of the Indiana Division, Indiana State Library and the staff of the Indiana Historical Society for aiding me in my search for records and photos.

And I want to thank some special friends who were particularly supportive: Elizabeth Steele Creveling, Edna M. Herman, Anne and Hayes O'Brien. And finally my family, Dave, David and Elise, have been absolutely the best support system any aspiring author could have. Thank you all.

Crown Hill

Though none of us will live forever, the stories can.
As long as one soul remains who can tell the story . . .

— Clarissa Pinkola Estes, *The Gift of Story*

Crown Hill Cemetery in Indianapolis, founded in 1863, is one of the largest cemeteries in the United States. This national historic landmark has over five hundred acres of landscaped lawns and native trees encircling the final resting places of President Benjamin Harrison and hundreds of Civil War dead. Many of my ancestors are also buried there, as are the ancestors of my husband, David Van Allen Fauvre. Someday we too will be buried in Crown Hill. We both want to continue the family tradition.

In 1965 my father, Bill Raffensperger, decided to buy a large burial plot at Crown Hill. He was fifty-two and a new grandfather. Though it was very important to him at the time, I really didn't want to listen to talk of cemetery plots. There was still some room in the Bauer family plot, that of his mother's family.

As my paternal grandmother was deeply loved by her sons and had been very significant to me as a child, I couldn't imagine why my father needed his own burial plot. I also thought he was making a ridiculously expensive purchase, electing to buy a ten thousand-dollar plot with space for twenty-four people!

But my father was adamant. He not only wanted a more beautiful plot than the Bauer's (his choice being a hillside location not far from my husband's family's), but he also wanted to erect a stone memorial engraved with his surname, Raffensperger. He told me the Bauer plot was nearly full and would have only room for his parents, himself and my mother, and his brother and his wife. It had no room for children or grandchildren.

I still saw no need for this new plot. My aunt and uncle, Ed and Alberta Raffensperger, had no children, and I was an only child. I had married in 1960, and had recently given birth to my first child, but

DAS DEUTSCHE HAUS (ATHENAEUM)

HOME OF FRANK M. FAUVRE

HOME OF EDWARD and FRANCES BRANHAM

WASHINGTON HALL
FIRST HOME OF THE MAENNERCHOR

HOME OF PHILIP SACHS

GERMAN-ENGLISH INDEPENDENT SCHOOL

H.C. RAFFENSPERGER DRUGS

KO-WE-BA BUILDING
BUILT 1924

KO-WE-BA FOODS

HOME OF GEORGE and MARY BAUER

FIRM OF BAUER and GOEPPER

GREENLAWN CEMETERY

WHITE RIVER

Indianapolis 1836–1924

N

my husband's family already had a large plot at Crown Hill. We would be buried there, I said. Husbands and wives were usually buried next to each other, I reminded Daddy.

We continued to argue, as we always had, but he did what I couldn't begin to appreciate at the time. He bought the plot. Five years later I again questioned my father's thinking. This man, whose intensity and perfectionism I tried so very hard to understand, did something I found very hard to accept.

Daddy asked his father Hiram J. Raffensperger to share the expense of erecting a Raffensperger monument. He also suggested that my grandfather be buried in the new plot and arrangements be made for the recently interred remains of my grandmother, Lucy Bauer Raffensperger, to be moved from the Bauer plot to the new Raffensperger plot. My parents' names were to be engraved on the base of the large monument; my grandparents would have stone markers in front of it. From my point of view, my father could have at least left all individual names off the monument using the surrounding headstones to tell the story of the Raffenspergers. But much to the disappointment of his eldest son, Edward, and to my surprise, my grandfather Hiram Raffensperger agreed to my father's plan.

My mother was pleased; her family had no plot at all. Now her parents would also be buried there in the new Raffensperger plot. I thought it all horribly egocentric and materialistic, even wasteful. I worried that my Bauer grandmother wouldn't like being moved from her family's historical burying ground. I didn't want my father to contemplate his own death, much less to die. I didn't want him to remind me that I too would eventually die. I didn't want anyone I loved to die. But of course they did.

It was at the knee of my beloved "Babboo," my name for Lucy Bauer Raffensperger, that I had been entertained for hours with the family history. Her stories emphasized our German American heritage dating back to 1836 when her great-grandparents emigrated to America. The Bauers had become important to me. I sensed their pride and appreciated their talent and dedication. I knew how devoted Babboo had been to her parents and sister. Still, devoted or not, in 1970, my grandmother's remains were moved from her Bauer family plot to the new

Raffensperger plot. Shortly thereafter, her in-laws, Charles and Katherine Howell, and then her husband of nearly sixty years, Hiram, joined her in death on my father's hill.

Lucy's youngest son and my father, George William Raffensperger, was buried on his hill in 1976. I was there for the internment that Bicentennial July, and it is a beautiful place. When I looked at the monument, the lush, grass covered hill and large-leafed oaks and tulip poplars, I thought of my father's foresight and pride and his need to be remembered. And I want him to be remembered.

The dates of my father's life, 1913-1976, are engraved on the lower half of the face of the Raffensperger monument. My mother's name and date of birth were engraved, as were my father's, when the stone was made. The date of her death was added in 1993. The monument is approximately ten feet wide, five feet high, and one foot thick, set vertically on a matching base. The stone is light grey granite, with "Raffensperger" carved across the face and again on the back in six-inch letters. The monument, elegant in its simplicity, is a tribute to my father's determination and good taste, both attributable, I think, to the German American qualities so instilled in him as a child.

I didn't want to talk about death with my father. I wanted him to live. But living became very difficult for him. His suicide came just eleven years after buying the Crown Hill plot and six years after erecting a monument to himself and his family.

When I look at the Fauvre family burial ground and then the Raffensperger's, the comparison is striking—big family versus small, old opposed to new, both tasteful but my father's more distinctive and contemporary. I can envision myself buried in the Raffensperger plot, but my husband, of course, can't. It really won't make much difference.

Babboo's marker was askew the late summer of 1990; that bothered me. It looked like the gophers of Crown Hill had burrowed a mound beneath it and somehow thrust the marker up several inches, exposing the bare earth beneath. My wonderful grandmother, who loved nature as well as family history would understand, but I didn't. I was angry; the gophers had left the Bauer plot undisturbed. Probably part of the first development of the cemetery, the Bauer plot is near a road, close to the street, one might say. My uncle Edward Raffensperger and his wife Alberta are buried there now, but no one would necessarily notice the Bauer plot when driving into the cemetery.

When we walked up the hill behind my mother's casket in March 1993, it was snowing. There were no leaves on the trees and the ground was muddy. A green tent covered the area around the Raffensperger monument, and a gray carpet covered the open grave and part of the ground where my father lies. Someone had placed two arrangements of red-orange gladiolas at the base of the monument. I thought how my mother hated orange and that roses or orchids would look prettier. I told myself I should have picked other arrangements to go to the cemetery but I reminded myself that no flowers, whatever the color, would last long in freezing weather. I looked at the casket and then the monument as the brief service was performed. I felt very sad, like a little girl again, and I wished that at least one of my relatives, now all lying in that hill, was there to comfort me. But at that moment, I also felt pride and a sense of gratitude that my father had made possible such a beautiful resting place for his family.

The Raffensperger plot, like that of the Fauvres, is on the way up to the James Whitcomb Riley Memorial, the highest point in the cemetery, perhaps the highest point in Indianapolis. Riley (1849-1916) was the poet laureate of Indiana. My grandmother remembered him fondly and told me he was a neighbor for a while when she was a child in Indianapolis. She and her sister had all of his books, some autographed. She read them to me when I was little and I read them to my children: "When the Frost is on the Punkin'," "The Raggedy Man," and "Little Orphant Annie." Riley wrote for the child's ear, but his rhyme and nineteenth-century Hoosier dialect is equally enjoyed by many an adult. In our library, I have my grandmother's first editions by James Whitcomb Riley, who resides uphill forever from Lucy and her family.

And nearby, on the winding road that takes you back into a less serene Indianapolis, are the plots of many German American families, who in death, as in life, continue to be bound by shared heritage, intermarriage, business partnerships, and sometimes by a sense of personal tragedy.

Babboo

A child becomes a man, and when he leaves he will take your
life with him.

— Wilbur Smith, *Power of the Sword*

When I was born in December of 1939, I was the first grandchild in the family. I was to be the only grandchild. I was taught, I assume, to call my grandmother and grandfather Babboo and Andad to replicate names Ed and Bill had called their grandparents, Bammo and Andad. "Babboo" and "Andad" were easy for me to say, and I called all four of my grandparents by these substitute names for Grandmother and Grandad. Babboo Raffensperger gave birth to two fine sons, but I became the little girl she never had.

When I was born, she was the same age I am now, fifty-five. From the moment of my birth, she was a commanding presence who subconsciously directed my life, expecting me to follow the traditions of the well known German American family from which she had come. A special bond grew between us, and though she has been gone for twenty-eight years, I still feel the warmth of her love and guidance. Perhaps now I appreciate her even more than I did growing up. I certainly have a better understanding of her life and the German American influence on that life in Indianapolis.

By the year of Babboo's birth, twenty years after the Civil War, the German community that had begun as early as 1840 in Indianapolis was well established, its organizations and leaders directing the growth of a city which numbered more than 75,000 inhabitants. Her paternal grandfather, along with Clemens Vonnegut and other German emigrants called "Forty-eighters," had helped in the founding of the Turners, the Maennerchor, the German-English Independent School, and the Republican Party in Indiana.

Babboo was born in Indianapolis in 1884, nearly fifty years after her paternal great-grandfather had emigrated from Germany and settled in the Hoosier capital. By the seventies and eighties the main street of town, Washington Street, was dominated by German businesses. By the nineties, ninety-one businesses from Delaware to Illinois Streets along Washington had German proprietors! Her grandfathers were pioneering merchants in the city: one a German emigrant, the other American-born. Her father, born in Indianapolis, was cofounder, with others of German heritage, of a distinguished wholesale grocery business. Her mother, a pianist, was active in the musical organizations of the city, helped found a needlework club, painted china, and wrote stories. Her sister, educated in Berlin, became a performing violinist in Indianapolis.

Babboo married Hiram Raffensperger, the son of a druggist born in Pennsylvania, and they had two sons. Lucy Raffensperger instilled in these sons the same values by which she had been raised, the values of the German American. Perseverance, accomplishment, cultural appreciation, business acumen and certainly family loyalty were all valued by those of German descent. The German Americans of her family's tradition dominated the life of early Indianapolis, contributing to the advancement and growth of the small city through their dedication to improving the educational system, organizing cultural opportunities, designing and building public buildings and being the leaders of the business community. When Lucy Bauer Raffensperger was born, the German influence in Indianapolis was at its zenith.

By 1884 Indianapolis, according to historian George Probst, "was far from modern according to present-day standards, but it did have nineteen miles of horse railroads on which fifty-nine cars operated. There was no longer just one block of pavement as in 1850 [when Lucy's grandparents arrived], but 211 miles of paved or gravelled streets, one mile of which was still in wood. Not over ten percent of the houses had water closets. Four theaters with stage appliances were found in the city; two of these were German-owned . . ." One of these was the Maennerchor Hall with a capacity of five hundred. With the love of music the Bauers possessed both through talent and cultivated taste, they were frequently performers and often part of the musical audience.

The year before Babboo's graduation from high school in 1903, the Indiana Soldiers and Sailors Monument was completed; its architects were two Germans. The monument, located on the Circle of downtown Indianapolis is one of the most imposing works of art in the state and was the largest Civil War memorial in the nation. As Babboo was watching the construction of this great monument, I doubt she dreamed that one day her son's offices would overlook it.

Like her parents and grandparents before her, Babboo watched the city grow and evolve, and as did her ancestors she knew the prominent people responsible for that growth. But family was more important to my grandmother than civic progress, and she treated hers with complete devotion. She also had a tremendous respect for nature and all living things and a commanding presence combined with a gentle nature. Fastidious and well organized, Babboo shared her mother's enjoyment of cooking, sewing and writing. And as my great-grandmother had, Babboo liked to travel. She enriched my life from the moment she told me the first of a trail of stories that went back three generations. She also instilled in me a sense of the importance of history, not only family history, but the history of our country. She admired and respected the Native American too and taught me to judge people by their characters, not the colors of their skins, their religions or ethnic backgrounds. Her creativity was boundless, as was her energy. She was my confidant, one of my best friends and a reliable constant in my life. But more than anything else, she was my teacher.

Her life, though perhaps not marked by greatness in the traditional sense, was nonetheless a testimony to her determination to overcome pain and loss with a strong faith in God and a fierce loyalty to family and friends. She had the wonderful ability to see the good in all things and in all people, never abandoning her marvelous sense of humor. She centered on people; conversation and communication were important to her. Babboo appreciated life, but more than all else she loved her family. That love shines through her writings as it does in her mother's.

Intellectually interesting, courageous people, Babboo's family believed in hard work, enterprise, and earning the respect of their neighbors, co-workers and friends. They believed in the importance of community, and they shared their talents and abilities to benefit that community. Fathers and mothers alike had high expectations for their children. It was hoped that each generation would build on the foundation built by the generation before it.

In this respect my family was not much different from other German American families in Indianapolis. All of these people shared heritage, language and, most of all, a strong desire to succeed. They often paid the price of success in an ethnic setting. The story of the Bauers and Raffenspergers is uniquely their own and the time feels right to tell it. In a manner much like Babboo told me long before I could really understand, I would like to share with you Babboo and Andad's family and mine.

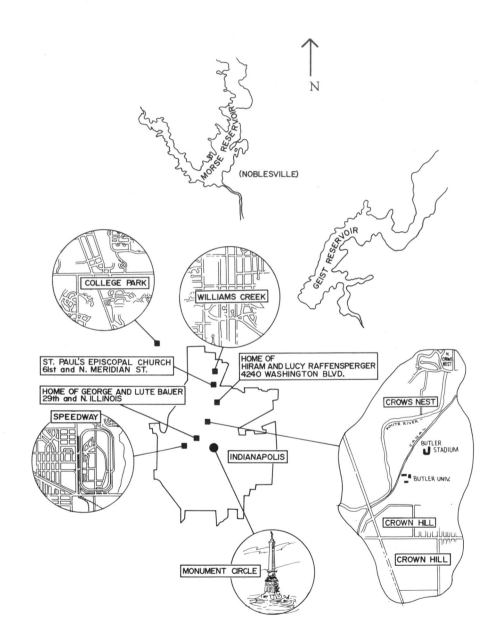

Greater Indianapolis area today.

The

Bauers

⚜ *The Bauers* ⚜

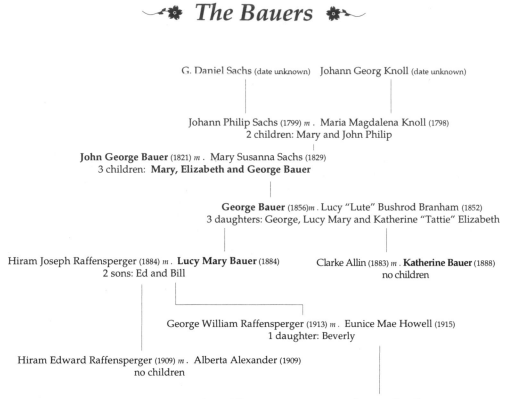

G. Daniel Sachs (date unknown)   Johann Georg Knoll (date unknown)

Johann Philip Sachs (1799) *m*. Maria Magdalena Knoll (1798)
2 children: Mary and John Philip

John George Bauer (1821) *m*. Mary Susanna Sachs (1829)
3 children: Mary, Elizabeth and George Bauer

George Bauer (1856)*m*. Lucy "Lute" Bushrod Branham (1852)
3 daughters: George, Lucy Mary and Katherine "Tattie" Elizabeth

Hiram Joseph Raffensperger (1884) *m*. Lucy Mary Bauer (1884)
2 sons: Ed and Bill

Clarke Allin (1883) *m*. Katherine Bauer (1888)
no children

George William Raffensperger (1913) *m*. Eunice Mae Howell (1915)
1 daughter: Beverly

Hiram Edward Raffensperger (1909) *m*. Alberta Alexander (1909)
no children

David Van Allen Fauvre (1938) *m*. Beverly Howell Raffensperger (1939)
2 children: David William and Cynthia Elise

Mary Sachs Bauer
(1829–1903)

The Bauer family was the fifth German family in Indianapolis, their history antedating even the typical story of major German American families in Indianapolis. They were a relatively small family. My children and I are their only living descendants. The Bauer women were educated and encouraged to use their creativity and talents; they were, indeed, almost as active as men in the community and certainly as loyal to their German American community.

My great-great-grandmother was Mary Sachs Bauer. Her birth certificate reads Maria Susanna Sachs, but she was called Mary in the United States. Mary Sachs was born in Hesse-Darmstadt, Germany, on Christmas Day, 1829. Hesse-Darmstadt, with Frankfort as its primary city, was one of the thirty-nine German states which made up the German Confederation established by the treaty of the Congress of Vienna in 1815. In the early 1800s Germany was less industrialized than other western European countries; most people earned their living as farmers and in cottage industries, German commerce and manufacturing being only in its infancy. Germans had little voice in their government. Though Hesse-Darmstadt was self-governing, most states were still ruled by kings or princes under their own laws, a situation with which Germans became increasingly dissatisfied.

Johann Philip Sachs, Mary's father, was one of the dissatisfied. Probably for economic reasons, he decided to come to America with his wife, Maria Magdalena Knoll Sachs, and their infant daughter. Philip Sachs, as he was called, was the son of G. Daniel Sachs, and was born in 1799 in Hessen, Germany. According to his passport, issued in 1830, he had blond hair and blue eyes. My grandmother told me that Philip Sachs was six feet nine inches tall, which is hard to believe considering the height of his descendants. I learned, however, that Philip had been most likely measured in "shoes" not feet. Measurements were not standardized in his day and a shoe size was that of the reigning prince. I imagine Philip was actually under six feet in height. His passport describes him as having a wide mouth, flatish nose and round face. Although he appeared healthy in coloring, his hair had begun to recede. Unfortunately, I don't have a photograph to verify this description. The passport also mentions that Philip Sachs could read, undoubtedly a skill not shared by many immigrants, though not unusual for German immigrants.

Philip Sachs brought to the United States a document which testifies to his exemplary military service for Hessen. He served for over eight years as a second guard and was regarded as a good, hard-working soldier, a man who knew when to obey and when to think independently. His civilian occupation was that of a weaver of fine textiles, such as linen. According to the translator of his military record, he was skilled in using a weaving machine. This record also noted that he was a Lutheran. When Philip and his small family left Germany, they traveled through cities west of the Rhine like Köln and Koblenz, many under French protection. Their ship departed from Amsterdam, Holland, in 1830.

Mary Sachs was six months old when her parents made this trip to America as part of the first wave of Germans who came for economic opportunity, not because of political pressures. At the time of their Atlantic crossing, Philip and Maria were both thirty-one. The trip took three months. The Sachs made their first home in Hagerstown, Maryland, and, while the family was living in Maryland in 1832, a son was born. He too was named John Philip Sachs.

Letters saved by his family indicate that Philip had cousins in Maryland. He corresponded with these cousins, usually in German, after moving West. In these letters his cousins described a life in Maryland that was hard, but not as difficult as life had been in their homeland. They encouraged other family members and friends to emigrate.

In 1836 the Sachs moved west to Indiana, making the journey overland in a wagon and settling in a home on East Market Street near the site of the old Jewish Temple in Indianapolis.

When Philip Sachs moved his small family from Maryland to what was called the West in 1836, the population of Indiana, which had acquired statehood in 1816, was approaching seven hundred thousand. Indianapolis was little more than a village. When his daughter Mary Sachs was ten years old, Indianapolis was a small town with a population of 2,692. By the time of her marriage to George Bauer in 1850, the population of Indianapolis had nearly quadrupled to 8,091. The majority of foreign-born immigrants in Indiana that same year were German. Germans settled in all parts of the state from Evansville on the Ohio River to South Bend, which had been an important trading post in the north; but fast-growing Indianapolis, named the capital in 1825, was a prime destination.

Mary watched the capital of Indiana grow into a major city and had the opportunity to associate with many of the prominent men and women who were responsible for that growth. The young woman was reported as having a very retentive memory; it was said that she knew every detail of Indianapolis' history.

The Sachs lived next door to Henry Ward Beecher (1813–1887), and the families became very close. Henry Ward Beecher, well known as both a dynamic Presbyterian preacher and author, served in Indianapolis between 1839 and 1847. Beecher was a member of the famous Beecher family: father Lyman, a New England clergyman known for his fiery sermons on temperance and opposition to Roman Catholicism, sister Catharine, an early supporter of education for women, and sister Harriet Beecher Stowe, an abolitionist and author of *Uncle Tom's Cabin*.

Apparently Philip Sachs did not pursue his weaving trade in Indianapolis. He served instead as the first sexton of the old City Cemetery commonly called Greenlawn after the 1870s. Established in 1821, Greenlawn (City) Cemetery was originally only twelve and half acres located on Kentucky Avenue between West Street and White River. The Greenlawn addition in 1838 increased the size to twenty-five acres. As sexton Philip was most likely responsible for the general care and upkeep of the cemetery. Philip was a Protestant and though raised a Lutheran, I suspect his family's friendship with their neighbors, the Beechers, which Mary's biographical obituary describes as "intimate" included their acceptance of Beecher's philosophy. Surely the Sachs very much admired Henry Ward Beecher; probably they attended his church, at least occasionally.

Beecher, who was determined to encourage intellectual flowering in the small pioneer town he had come to serve, was well educated. He had graduated from Amherst College before attending Lane (Presbyterian) Seminary in Ohio, where his father Lyman was its first President from 1832–1850. Interestingly, both Lyman and Henry became Congregational clergymen after serving the Presbyterian Church for many years. Like his sister Harriet, Henry was a prolific writer. Near the end of his life, when he had returned to New England, he wrote *Evolution and Religion* (1885) as an attempt to reconcile evolution and the Bible. He brought these interests to an Indianapolis just beginning to cultivate literary societies, lyceums, philosophical societies and libraries. German community expression was part of that flowering.

Philip and Maria Sachs lived in Indianapolis until their deaths in 1856 at the ages of fifty-seven and fifty-six. Originally buried in Greenlawn Cemetery, their remains and those of other Sachs family members were moved to Crown Hill Cemetery in 1896. Their headstones, along with those of daughter Mary Sachs Bauer, are in the Bauer family plot which was purchased by their grandchildren in 1895. These earliest pioneers left a loyal family which promoted German culture and thought in their adopted city. Mary Sachs grew up to be a respected and beloved citizen of Indianapolis. The *Indianapolis Trade Journal* reported that she had a lifelong interest in civic affairs, particularly in the German community, but was perhaps best known for her kindly ministrations to the sick and afflicted. She married another German, George Bauer, in 1850.

(John) George Bauer
(1821-1858)

George Bauer, first name John, Mary Sachs' future husband, was born in Neckardenzlingen, Wuerttemberg, Germany, December 31,1821.

"Intolerable economic conditions in the German states and a desire for betterment in as short a time as possible was one of the primary causes for the coming of the Germans to America," says George T. Probst in his book *The Germans in Indianapolis 1840–1918*. He goes on to say:

> *Authoritarian German government was another factor which caused many Germans to leave their native country. The governments of the German states were headed by princes who refused to be bound by democratic constitutions. There had been demonstrations and uprisings in the 1820s and 1830s by the liberal-minded element . . . But the revolutions in the various German states during 1848 proved to many of the liberal-minded Germans that change in their Fatherland was an impossibility at that time. Discouraged . . . many of these "Forty-eighters," as the revolutionists came to be known, left the country in disgust and set sail for America. A number of these victims of political persecution found their way into the little village of Indianapolis, where not a few became leaders in the community. (pp. 5–6)*

George Bauer was a "Forty-eighter," a liberal in spirit though he arrived in America in 1846. In 1848 he settled in Indianapolis and became a naturalized American citizen in 1856. In 1850 George, twenty-nine, married Mary Sachs, twenty-one. They were undoubtedly drawn to one another by their common German heritage. George was at the time a merchant tailor in business with another German, Frederick Goepper, and an advertisement in the *Indiana Daily State*

Sentinel describes Bauer & Goepper as "merchant tailors and dealers in ready made clothing and furnishing goods, No. 21 West Washington Street, opposite the *Sentinel* office."

The Bauers' home, a brick double house at about the 100 block of North Illinois Street, between Market and Ohio streets, was owned by the firm of Bauer & Goepper. In 1850 the house was the farthest north in the city. The birthplace of one or two of their children, this home was on the site of the Lyric Theatre of the twentieth century. Probst continues:

> *The Forty-eighters were of a different spirit in politics and religion than many of the established German families, and they were organizers and leaders in the community. They lost no time after their arrival in founding organizations through which they could express themselves and plan a course of action in challenging some of the existing ideas of their day.* (p. 21)

One of the many Forty-eighters who became prominent in Indianapolis and active in its cultural affairs was Herman Lieber, who founded a picture frame factory and art gallery. In 1880, the year of George's son's marriage, Lieber headed a group of investors who financed promising Indiana artist T. C. Steele's study in Munich. After five years, Steele and his family returned to their native state and repaid his debt to these supporters by painting their portraits. Today T. C. Steele is considered one of the foremost American impressionists and his art is beloved by all who are Hoosier. In 1945 T. C. Steele's great-granddaughter, Elizabeth Steele, and George Bauer's great-great granddaughter, Beverly Raffensperger, found themselves as children living across the street from one another. Had it not been for the influence of Forty-eighters on the city of Indianapolis our friendship of now some fifty years might never have happened.

One of the groups founded by the Forty-eighters in the Hoosier capital was an Anti-Monarchy Society, supporting European Germans in their efforts to establish a free government. In Indiana, the *Freimaenner Verein*, or Association of Freemen, was an organization dedicated to the abolition of slavery and determined to fight against any prejudice, political or religious. The Freemen were not willing to keep their opinions among themselves; they actively pursued their goals through the press and public debate, as they attempted to educate their community in liberal thought.

George Bauer was a prominent member of the Freimaenner Verein and most likely a participant in the Freemen's state convention held in Indianapolis in 1854. Outspoken abolitionists supporting the Republican philosophy, the society expressed its views in the radical German *Freie Presse*, one of the two German weekly newspapers in Indianapolis in the 1850s. The *Freie Presse*, printed in German, was continually published until the close of the Civil War. German was the universal language until about 1865 in Indianapolis' German neighborhoods; after the Civil War English began to be a second tongue spoken in the homes of German families.

The Freemen, dedicated as they were to promoting their philosophy through education, felt the need for a school with higher standards than those available at the time. Although free schools had been mandated in Indiana in 1850, public education in mid-nineteenth century Indianapolis was erratic at best. In August, 1859, for example, the *Indianapolis Journal* reported that the public schools could not be opened before February, 1860. In addition, the public schools had refused to hire a teacher of German for that segment of the city's population. George Bauer and his partner Frederick Goepper, along with others in the German community, laid the groundwork for the establishment of the German-English Independent School of Indianapolis.

The German-English School Society was formed to promote and raise funds to build a private school. Clemens Vonnegut, who founded the Vonnegut Hardware Company and was one of the most prominent German Americans in Indianapolis, was elected president of the Society and was continuously reelected until the school closed. Born in Prussia, Vonnegut had emigrated to America in 1848 and settled in Indianapolis in 1850, where he was undoubtedly befriended by George Bauer and others in the German community. Clemens was the great-grandfather of the popular American author, Kurt Vonnegut, Jr. (Kurt and my husband David share common cousins, Frank Fauvre

Vonnegut and Henry Schnull Fauvre.) Henry Fauvre was named for his maternal ancestor, Henry Schnull, another prominent Forty-eighter, who was a wholesale grocer and banker in post Civil War Indianapolis.

The purpose of the German-English Independent School of Indianapolis was to educate children in both the German and English languages independent of *all* sectarian influence: most German Free-thinkers objected to both the orthodox and more liberal varieties of organized Christianity. Though some fellow citizens thought them "infidels," these freethinking German immigrants went their own way and opened their school in May of 1860.

Germans in Indianapolis did know how to have fun and they loved celebrations. In 1866 German families held a pageant and festival on the Fourth of July to raise money for a new German-English school building that was underway on the original land and an adjacent lot. July 4 was a special holiday anyway; as soon as the German families had set foot on American soil they made it plain that while they still loved the traditions of the Fatherland, they were going to be solid Americans. Many German American Hoosiers died in the Civil War so the celebration was particularly meaningful. The parade featured wagons with various tableaux from organizations such as the Octavian Grove of Druids, the Teutonic Oddfellows, and the Maennerchor.

George Probst reported that after the parade twenty thousand people gathered to hear the reading of the Declaration of Independence and picnic. There was dancing, plenty of beer and a concert by the Maennerchor. It is unfortunate that George Bauer couldn't have attended such a happy celebration benefiting the German-English School which meant so much to him.

Until the school they funded closed in 1882, it was located on the north side of Maryland Street between Delaware and Alabama streets.

Theodore Stein's book, *Our Old School*, describes George Bauer:

One of the most enterprising and public spirited of our citizens of German birth. He was not only recognized as an honorable and upright gentleman, but he was a leader in the thought and part of the leaven which brought about the organization of the Republican party in this locality, so far as the German population was concerned. His children, Elizabeth, Mary, and George, were pupils of our old school from its inception, and one regret is that their father did not live to see the fruit of his labors ripen . . .

Both George and Mary Bauer are pictured in *Our Old School*, with Mary's photograph in the section entitled "Women Who Aided the School." Mr. Stein credits Misses Lizzie and Mary Bauer, George and Mary's daughters, for assisting him in researching the roster of former pupils of the German-English Independent School prior to the book's publication in 1914. In looking over the list of one thousand names (which Stein says is unfortunately incomplete), I found the name of my husband's grandfather, Frank A. (Maus) Fauvre.

Frank's father, Caspar Maus, emigrated to America in 1835 from Alsace-Lorraine and was one of the early pioneers of Dearborn County. After marrying in Cincinnati, he and his wife settled in New Alsace where in 1842 he erected the first steam grist mill in eastern Indiana. While his older sons served in the Union Army, Caspar served his county as an enrolling officer, drafting soldiers for the Union. In 1863 his mill was destroyed by fire by Confederate sympathizers. The family moved to Indianapolis where he founded the C. Maus brewery and sent his children to the German-English Independent school.

Frank Maus Fauvre, Dave's grandfather, studied law before joining his older brothers in the management of the family brewery. Because of the Republican support at the time for Prohibition, he joined the Democratic Party and represented the party on the City Council between 1876 and 1880. In 1889 the Maus, Schmidt, and Lieber breweries were sold to an English syndicate and merged to form the Indianapolis Brewing Company.

After the sale of the brewery, Frank became an investor with numerous interests, but first he took steps to change the family name. Though French in origin, Maus was constantly pronounced in the German manner, *mouse* instead of *moss*. In 1900 Frank chose to change the name to that of his paternal grandmother's maiden name, Favre. A "u" was added to make the pronunciation easier.

Frank Maus Fauvre built and operated the first artificial ice company in Indianapolis and served as president of People's Light and Heat Company. Between 1902 and 1905 Frank was part owner and president of the first Interurban Rail System and he owned and operated the Fauvre Coal Company, which later consolidated with the German American Trust Company, (Fletcher Trust). This entrepreneur had extensive real estate holdings as well, including the Marion Building, which stood on the corner of North Meridian and Ohio streets, now the site of Ameritech, and also the land beneath the Circle Tower Building.

Indianapolis is proud to have the oldest continuously existing male chorus in the United States, and, interestingly, the Indianapolis Maennerchor played an important role both in the life and death of George Bauer. The history of the Maennerchor is traced to 1854 when four of the Forty-eighters occupied a third-floor room at 75 East Washington Street, for which they paid three dollars a month. Lacking any other entertainment the German immigrants, accompanied by a guitarist, began to sing the old songs of their homeland together, and soon they attracted other men who liked to sing.

Among the third-floor frequent visitors was George Bauer. His loyalty to the Maennerchor and it to him was underscored finally upon the occasion of his unfortunate and premature death at the age of thirty-seven. George Bauer suffered from an affliction involving his throat, possibly a goiter. After traveling to Cincinnati to have surgery, he died in 1858, only eight years after his marriage to Mary Sachs, leaving her with three young children. He was held in such high regard by his family and friends in Indianapolis, about a hundred and sixty miles away, that they traveled to Cincinnati to receive his body and celebrate his life. Along with his family, committees from the Maennerchor, Oddfellows, and his exercise club accompanied his coffin, which was carried on a wagon drawn by two white horses. As the procession with its group of German mourners walked alongside the wagon to the train depot, the Maennerchor sang. After George's body was returned to Indianapolis his friends thanked their compatriots in Cincinnati for their support in the *Cincinnati Republikanner*.

George's Turner club, the Indianapolis Turnergemeinde, had been organized by August Hoffmeister, Jacob Metzger, John Ott, Karl Hill and Clemens Vonnegut. The Turners were inspired by Friedrich Ludwig Jahn (1778–1852) a physical exercise enthusiast who advocated a complete program for physical and mental health in Germany. Political and social questions became part of the format, with the Turners promoting civil rights in Germany. The most radical were those who came to the United States seeking political freedom and recreated the exercise program in their new country. The efforts and methods of the Indianapolis Turners were influential in the establishment of a physical education program in the Indianapolis school system.

In 1894 Das Deutsche Haus was built by the Turners for the purpose of providing a building for social gatherings, gymnastics, and assemblies of the liberal-minded German element of the city. (The name Das Deutsche Haus was changed to the Athenaeum because of anti-German sentiment during World War I.) In 1893 the "Southside Turverein" (a Turner organization serving the southside of Indianapolis) was founded with Diedrich Mussman as president. Diedrich had emigrated from Bremen, Germany, where he and his family owned and operated an ironworks in 1872. The Mussmann ironworks cast bells for churches until the Franco-Prussian war, when they began making cannons. As the French were more in need of cannon, they chose to sell to them. However, the Germans won the war, so the Mussmanns left their homeland. Diedrich had a lumberyard on the southwest corner of Morris and Meridian streets and a brickyard in Noblesville, before becoming associated with the Coal Motor Car Company.

In 1937 the Maennerchor came to have its home in the Athenaenum. I don't remember the Maennerchor, but I remember the Athenaenum from my childhood days. An imposing building at Michigan and New Jersey Streets, the Athenaenum included club rooms, a large ballroom, auditorium, gymnasium, restaurant, bar and of course a "Biergarten." My grandparents were members and took me there as a young child for German dinners. At the time I had no idea of its historical significance to my family. The Athenaeum-Das Deutsche Haus is very much alive and well in 1995, and the building is being restored to its original grandeur. The gymnasium, which looks much as it did at the turn of the century, is now used by the YMCA. George Bauer would undoubtedly have joined Clemens Vonnegut, Henry

Schnull and others in supporting the Turner movement and the building of such a monument to German culture and philosophy. He would have been proud of the accomplishments of his fellow Forty-eighters. His premature death kept him from experiencing the satisfaction of seeing the huge building that became the crowning achievement of German American pride in the 1890s.

Rearing three children alone during the Civil War must have been difficult for Mary Sachs Bauer, but she managed, probably with the help of family and friends, to bring to adulthood three well educated and successful children. Mary's obituary in the *Indianapolis Trade Journal* reported that she "took a lively interest in young people and numbered hosts of them as her friends." Mary lived to be seventy-four. Her younger brother John Philip Sachs, who was a cooper by trade, may have been a support to her. I do not know his history, nor remember my grandmother ever mentioning him. John lived to be eighty-seven and is buried near his parents, George and Mary, in the Bauer plot in Crown Hill Cemetery.

George Bauer, Sr., and his German friends were enthusiastic immigrants. Culturally alive, they prided themselves on being freethinkers and many of them were members of the newly important Republican Party. They enriched their adopted country.

John G. Rauch could have been describing the lives of my great-great-grandparents and their friends when he wrote:

> *The exodus of Germans started about 1820—first a trickle and then a mighty river, until by 1890 the census figures of that year disclosed that six and one-half million Germans crossed the ocean and settled mostly in the Midwest . . . The aristocrats, merchants and masters of Germany naturally were satisfied with their privileges and did not emigrate; but the peasants and journeymen brought their precious skills and industry with them and in less than a century brought the Midwest from a wilderness to the most highly developed economic area which the world has ever known. It will always remain a veritable miracle.*

George Bauer, Jr., and His Sisters, Mary and Elizabeth Bauer

George and Mary Sachs Bauer had three children who survived infancy: Mary, Elizabeth, and George. A second son, John (also named for his father), was born in 1858, and died the following year. George Bauer, my great-grandfather, was the youngest of the three surviving Bauer children. Born in 1856, he was two at the time of his father's death and grew up in a household of three women. Like his sisters, he was educated at the German-English Independent School already described. His friends were also raised in the German community, as he was, the sons and daughters of German immigrants. George did not follow his father's merchant tailoring trade. Upon completion of his studies at the remarkable age of fourteen, he accepted a position with Isaiah Mansur, who owned a private bank at Washington and Alabama streets. At age twenty-five, George went with the firm of Schnull & Krag, wholesale grocers. Schnull & Co., established in 1855, was the first wholesale grocery company in Indianapolis.

Co-salesmen at Schnull & Krag were William Kothe and Charles Wells. The three men were apparently vocal in their criticism of company policies. Schnull, according to former Ko-We-Ba president Al Gisler, Jr., told Kothe, Wells and Bauer that if they didn't like the way he ran things, they could start their own company!

Having worked for Schnull & Krag for eight years, George Bauer, Jr. at age thirty-three, joined the Kothe brothers and Charles Wells to found a new wholesale grocery business with offices at 128 and 130 South Meridian Street. They were among a group of Germans who had prospered and saved their money and were looking beyond Washington Street; they needed large manufacturing and commercial buildings for the post Civil War business boom. These new enterprises including the wholesale grocery were located in the "Commercial District" Henry Schnull planned: just south of Washington Street.

Like George, George and William Kothe were also the sons of a Forty-eighter; their father, William, had arrived in Indianapolis in 1851. The four founders divided the responsibilities. George Kothe was the financier. William was in charge of buying and inside sales. George Bauer and Charles Wells were the traveling salesmen. Initially the company sold only within a forty-mile radius of Indianapolis, but their sales territories grew quickly.

In 1934 William Kothe recalled the early days of Ko-We-Ba for *The Indianapolis Star*. "There really was not a good street in town. Washington street was paved with cobblestones. It was terrible. We would rather have had a dirt road. The street was a mountain in the center and it sloped precipitously to both gutters. In the winter, if you weren't careful, you'd slip off the center and slide down into the gutter."

No semitrailers brought loads to the supermarket back door in the 1890s; the method of food distribution and business practices were very different. William Kothe said

> Mr. Wells would leave Indianapolis at 4 o'clock Monday morning. He would go by train to Edinburgh, where he would hire a team and buggy. First he would drive to Taylorsville and then to Columbus, reaching the latter city late on Monday. There were a lot of German grocers in Columbus then. On Monday evening they would gather somewhere with Mr. Wells for an evening of gossip and perhaps beer. On Tuesday he would spend the entire day calling upon his customers. He took no orders, however. It was mainly a series of friendly calls. That evening there would be another friendly gathering somewhere, and on Wednesday he would really begin to transact business.
>
> Mr. Bauer's procedure was similar. He also would leave Indianapolis at 4 o'clock on Monday morning and would go by train to Fortville, where he would engage a 'rig.' For three days he would drive through that section of the state behind a team, continuing north of Muncie. Any one of our ten salesmen now [1934] could make the same territory that Mr. Bauer covered within one day and have some leisure time left afterward.

At the turn of the century Hyman's *Handbook of Indianapolis* published this description of Ko-We-Ba:

> *An important member of the wholesale grocery trade of Indianapo-
> lis is the house of Kothe, Wells & Bauer, composed of William Kothe,
> Charles W. Wells and George Bauer . . . organized in January, 1889.
> The firm is located in the heart of the wholesale trade district where they
> occupy a handsome four-story building, 35 by 150 feet, and containing
> all modern facilities and improvements for the storage, display, sale and
> shipment of stock and the transaction of business. The firm's warehouse
> is located at the corner of Delaware and Merrill streets, where the large
> reserve stock is carried.*

> *They carry full lines of staple and fancy groceries, making special-
> ties of teas, coffees and sugars of the choicest grades and varieties. In
> their department of fancy groceries they include canned and potted meats,
> fruits and preserves, sauces, pickles, spices, baking powders, etc., also
> handling the best brands of smoking and chewing tobaccos and cigars,
> with other articles appertaining generally to the business.*

> *The goods packed specially by this house and known by the brand
> of "Ko-We-Ba" are sold under a guarantee to give satisfaction or money
> refunded, and no goods sold in this market have a greater reputation for
> superior quality and absolute purity. The house has a large trade through-
> out Indiana, Ohio, Illinois, Michigan, Kentucky, and Pennsylvania,
> which is visited regularly by 10 traveling men. The members of the firm
> are men of enterprise and business ability.*

George Bauer's sisters, Mary and Elizabeth (later called Aunt Liz
or Lizzie), never married. They were both professional women. Mary,
the youngest, born in 1854, was a saleswoman for Charles Mayer and
Co. "Charlie" Mayer had opened his toy and notions store in 1840; it
later became a household furnishings and fine gift store, but they always carried some top quality toys. The store was still in business when
I was a little girl, over a hundred years after its founding. It was down
on Washington Street near L. S. Ayres. I well remember that only

"Charlie Mayer" carried my favorite dolls manufactured in Lincoln, Nebraska. Now collectors' favorites, they were called the "Terry and Jerry" dolls and had a complete line of clothes long before "Barbie" became every little girl's dream.

I was too young to remember Aunt Mary Bauer, but I certainly remember the store where she worked. It was a beautiful, old store; it had remained the same for three generations. Charles Mayer's impressive emporium was three or four stories tall; the second story had a mezzanine which overlooked the main floor. Beneath the counters was dark stained library paneling. The countertops were also wood; the shelves and cases, glass. An old fashioned cage-style elevator carried customers to upper floors and money was exchanged via the mysterious system of pneumatic tubes. The old store finally closed its doors in 1954, thirty-one years after the death of Mary Bauer.

Elizabeth Bauer was a highly respected assistant to insurance agents in Indianapolis. She was born in a house on Ohio street just off Bird Street in 1851. The family moved when she was quite young to Illinois Street where there were residences all around them, but Elizabeth recalled:

> As the city began to grow our neighbors began to move. Their houses were torn down and business places were built. We didn't want to move and were among the last to do so, but I well remember that we finally were pretty well hemmed in, with a saloon on each side of us.

On the occasion of her eightieth birthday in 1931 Elizabeth Bauer was interviewed for a story in *The Indianapolis News*. At the time she was still working for an insurance agent as she had for fifty-two years! She was colorfully described as "unwrinkled, bright-eyed, and slim" with "pep and alert-sprightliness!" In the article Aunt Liz reminisced about her early days in the business world:

> I clerked in a dry goods store and in a shoe store before that. The dry goods store was where the Terminal Station is now and handled fine laces, ribbons and trimmings of various kinds. All my salary went back into the store for those laces and ribbons, too. I lived right across from

the store, which sounds almost unbelievable today. Our old home stood where the Lyric theater is now.

Illinois street did not look then as it does now. No, indeed. It was a cobble stone street and no street cars traveled up and down it. There were hitching posts here and there along it. My father and mother were both German born. My father came here after he was grown, although my mother was only a baby when her parents brought her over. Father came with his partner from Germany and started a tailor shop where the State Life building stands. I went to a private school at the southwest corner of Washington and Alabama streets and the old building is still there [German-English Independent School].

Solicitors drove horses hitched to buggies. When they would go on their vacations, I would frequently substitute in soliciting for them and I would drive over town in a trap. I could drive a horse anywhere, but I never did have a desire to drive a car, so I have arrived at this mature age without owning an automobile.

As a single professional woman Aunt Liz lived alone in a two-story house at 3904 Carrollton Avenue, which would have been out in the country when she was a beginning her long career in downtown Indianapolis, four or so miles south. My mother remembered that she and my father spent Thanksgiving once with Aunt Liz before their marriage. She had a rather formidable personality, Mother thought, and she described her as "business-like, stiff—rather masculine." Nonetheless, Aunt Liz was cordial that holiday.

Aunt Liz died at age eighty-three. The announcement of her death in *The Indianapolis News*, September 9, 1935, stated that she had taken ill only hours before her death. It also noted that before retiring at age eighty, she had worked for Franklin Fire, John Wocher, Aetna and Robert Collier fire insurance companies. Elizabeth Bauer was also a member of the Maennerchor, like her father who helped found the Indianapolis institution. She sang with the German House choir. After her death my uncle, Ed Raffensperger, and his wife, Alberta, lived in her home for awhile.

Aunt Liz was a remarkable woman and fifty years ahead of her time. I marvel at her courage and independence. Perhaps the masculinity my mother saw in her was the toughness Elizabeth Bauer had to develop to survive in a man's world before World War II. She and Aunt Mary may well have inherited their independent spirit from their mother, Mary Sachs, who never remarried after the untimely death of her husband when she was only twenty-nine years old.

But younger brother George Bauer, Jr., would not remain a bachelor. He married Lucy Bushrod Branham in March of 1880. He was twenty-four and Lucy was twenty-eight. It's likely they met through their families, because Lucy was the daughter of another wholesale merchant, Edward Branham.

John Rauch wrote, "Though the Germans retained their language and promoted their cultural heritage for the first generation or two, they didn't force their preferences on their neighbors. Sharing their common origin in the Teutonic tribes of Western Europe, they identified most with the English in America." Both the English and German emigrants, Rauch continues, "were intelligent, literate, industrious and fastidious in their patterns of living. They immediately intermarried and became very soon completely assimilated. There is hardly a prominent Midwestern family today which is not, to a greater or lesser degree, an amalgam of English and German ancestors." George Bauer was a good example. Though both his parents had been born in Germany and supported the German organizations of early Indianapolis, George married a longtime American of primarily English heritage.

Lucy "Lute" Bushrod Branham Bauer
(1852–1920)

Babboo had handsome mahogany bedroom furniture. One piece I particularly admired was her mirrored vanity table. I remember her brushing her hair while sitting in front of it. In the center of the vanity sat her cut glass jars with engraved silver lids for powder and hair pins. On one side of the vanity table Babboo always displayed three small gold frames containing pictures of her family: her father, George Bauer, her sister, Katherine Bauer Allin, and her mother, Lucy Bushrod Branham Bauer, commonly called "Lute." It was hard for me as a child to imagine this serious looking group of Bauers as the loved ones of my sweet and cheerful grandmother. Lute's portrait portrays her as a plump middle-aged woman with brown hair pulled back in a loose bun from a round face. There is no smile and she looks sad.

Although my grandmother often spoke of her family, they were all deceased by the time I was born, so I never met the Bauers. I imagine I would have been a little intimidated if I had. There is a physical resemblance between mother, Lute, and daughter, Lucy Mary. They were both short, rounded women. My grandmother couldn't have been taller than four feet eleven inches. Both were buxom. My grandmother was the more attractive woman with gorgeous dark eyes and her father's sophisticated nose.

Babboo's grandfather Edward Branham came from Madison, Indiana, and married Frances Taylor, the daughter of Madison's popular judge, William McKendrick Taylor. Judge Taylor was born in Kentucky, where he studied law before making Madison his home in 1825. At the time, the Ohio river town had a population of about six thousand and homes were mostly made of logs. Judge Taylor served Madison in numerous municipal capacities including Mayor, and according to newspaper accounts was beloved by his adopted community. William Taylor died in Madison during the Civil War, but his wife, Mary Jane Wallace Taylor, survived him by twenty-eight years, dying in Indianapolis at the age of eighty-two.

Edward and Frances Taylor Branham moved to Indianapolis in 1864, when the antebellum community of Madison was faced with a declining trade area and a reduction in river traffic. Railway lines had begun to favor Madison's main urban competitors, Cincinnati, Louisville, and Indianapolis. Edward was one of the pioneer wholesale merchants of south Meridian Street, having established himself in the wholesale shoe business as a young man in Madison. His firm's name was A. B. Smith & Co. Later he partnered with E. C. Mayhew and established a wholesale shoe and boot store under the name of Mayhew and Branham. A few years after that the partnership was dissolved. The business became known as McKee & Branham Wholesale Boots and Shoes and remained active for many years. Like Ko-We-Ba Foods, it was located in the wholesale district of the city on South Meridian Street.

Lute Branham's brother Edward T. Branham started working at McKee and Branham after high school. With Mr. McKee as his boss, he began as a porter and packer but in time he traveled, usually by train, to sell the line of shoes to stores around the state. Ed Branham wrote of the early life of the Branham family in Indianapolis in an autobiography published by friends after his death in 1946:

> We lived in Indianapolis, then known as a "city of homes." Our house was in old Tennessee Street (now Capitol Avenue) at the corner of Michigan Street. It was a large house with rooms enough to accommodate father, mother, and six children. An extra room for visitors was usually occupied.
>
> Father wasn't rich, but he always had enough and was very generous, so the financial problem didn't brother us.
>
> The home of those days was headquarters for all the activities of life. There were no telephones, radios, automobiles, movies, or public dances. Pleasures and recreation were supplied in the homes. Each home, if possible, had the top floor equipped for parties and dances. These events furnished a large part of our social life.

Lute Branham was the eldest of the six Branham children; she was twenty-eight when she married George Bauer in 1880. It seems strange in that era that Lute waited so long to marry, but as an extremely talented and creative woman, I suspect her days were busy and involved with her large family and friends. Lute was also a pianist. Betty Davenport Humston remembered her great aunt and wrote me, " Mother told me about seeing and hearing her piano accompaniment for your great-aunt Katherine Bauer and her violin. Aunt Lute lacked the long, slender fingers of some pianists, but Mother said her short, plump ones fairly flew all over the keyboard, and she was a wonderful accompanist."

Lute was thirty-one when she gave birth to her first child in Indianapolis in 1883, her daughter—*George!* Husband George had wished for a son and stubbornly insisted on naming the baby girl George despite pleas from Lute to use a more feminine version of the name. Sadly, baby George died in 1883 and is buried in the Branham plot at Crown Hill Cemetery. My grandmother, who was born the following year, never mentioned her deceased older sister to me. Christened Lucy Mary, my grandmother was named for her mother and probably her father's sister. Three years later, in 1887, a third daughter, Katherine Elizabeth, was born. Both surviving daughters were quite musically talented like their mother. My grandmother Lucy played the piano and organ while her younger sister Katherine (who became known as "Tattie") studied to be a concert violinist.

Lute's talents were multifaceted. Not only did she play the piano, she also was adept at china painting, a popular hobby of the day. She left a legacy of beautiful dessert plates decorated with flowers and in some instances the autographs of family members. Lute was also an excellent seamstress. I have inherited monogrammed linens that were embroidered by her and her gold thimble engraved with her name. In association with her sewing skills, she cofounded the "Long Thread Needle Club" about which she wrote a short history that I have excerpted below. This history shows the sense of humor not visible in her photographs. She had married into a German American family, and her life demonstrated the richly interesting life German American women enjoyed at the turn of the century in the Hoosier Capital.

Once upon a time—many years ago—although not beyond the memory of the earliest inhabitant, there was a village-like addition to the City of Indianapolis, north of Fall Creek, whose inhabitants seemed all-sufficient unto themselves. They were too congenial to drift apart, so they conceived the happy idea of forming a club, a needle club, to meet fortnightly. Not to be selfish in this pleasure, they extended a few guarded invitations to some not north of the creek [friends who lived south of Fall Creek] to join them.

The club was christened "The Long Thread Needle Club," by John Orin Spahr, who bears the distinction of being the only man to butt into the affairs of the club. When the needle club first started, it was in reality very much like an embroidery class with Mrs. J. O. Spahr as teacher. She was expected to solve all color schemes, untie all knotty problems in the embroidery floss world, and supervise everything that every one else essayed to do, to the neglect of her own work. All this she did so good-naturedly that we all worked hard to be able to stand on our own feet, and let her have peace. This we have accomplished, in a way, and now have a mutual admiration society for each other's work.

I have always contended that the reason the needle club has continued all these years is because we have no parliamentary rules, no officers, and all make pretty things for ourselves and friends. People sew industriously by spells, for church and charity, but making aprons, caps, broom covers and dish towels, is sure to grow monotonous as the years go on, and all of us love dainty, beautiful work, so our charity work is done on the side. Are we selfish in this? I think not, for we do not keep our treasures to ourselves.

Are we congenial? Most assuredly we are, and a fun-loving lot. Our jokes are tellable, our gossip harmless, and our arguments good-natured. I have a picture in my mind of the far distant future. On a certain day, every fortnight, wheelchairs may be seen coming to a given point, from all directions. A stranger asks: "What occasion is this? Some pleasant jubilee, certainly, for all these little old ladies look so bright with anticipation, their false teeth and specs polished so bright, and their dear old hands clutching lovingly their fancy work-bags." Then shall the answer be:

" 'Tis a regular meeting of the Long Thread Needle Club, the most exclusive of clubs in the city, years ago closed to all new members but posterity."

Lute Bauer wrote these proud words at the age of sixty-two. It comes as no surprise that she was asked to be historian. She loved to write.

My father and uncle were Lute's only grandchildren; I am her only great-grandchild. Because I am, I have inherited her writings and letters. They are all impressive in their grammar and style.

Apparently Lucy B. B. Bauer did not aspire to be a published author. She was content, I assume, to write for the pleasure of her family. Although women like Louisa May Alcott, Harriet Beecher Stowe, and George Eliot had achieved prominence by 1890, women authors were still frowned on in polite society. Lute's writing often took the form of charming and clever books, created for her daughters and nieces. She made my grandmother Lucy and cousins Nancy and Rene Ohr similar alphabet books. These books, now with disintegrating cloth covers, were entitled: "To Lucy's Friends and Cousins." Both books are "Affectionately Dedicated by Aunt Lute," and dated February 14, 1887. The alphabet letters and poems are printed neatly in black ink and illustrated with the wonderfully romantic turn-of-the century paper cutouts, colorful ones printed on heavy glossy paper which were often used for Valentines and Christmas cards. Many of the rhymes are personalized:

> *G is for Grandma and Grossmama too.*
> *H is for Hands, two for me, two for you*
> *I is Miss Ida as big as a minute.*
> *J is a Jug, I wonder what's in it?*
> *K is Aunt Katie who loves her two nieces.*
> *L is for Lucy who'd squeeze her to pieces.*
> *M is for Mazie so fat and sweet.*
> *N is for Negro. You can't see his feet.*

(The accompanying picture shows only the upper body of a black child. His hands are raised and he looks expectant, like maybe he is waiting to receive something, or catch a ball.)

After her alphabet poem Lute included short poems like these two:

Mazie and Lucy are two little girls
One has straight hair, one has curls.
One has brown eyes, one has gray
Both do love to romp and play.

Mazie has a black doll, name is "Sue"
Lucy's "Shinah" is a black doll too.

Lute Bauer was a prolific writer. Besides her history of the club and her alphabet books, I am fortunate to possess several other examples of her writing, all in her own hand, a most attractive and readable script. Her inspiration obviously was her two daughters and five nieces. Her brother, Edward Taylor Branham, had five girls! I have two small blue books with red binding. One, *Alice,** is a story about her niece, Alice Branham, on the occasion of the birth of Alice's cousin, Katherine Elizabeth Bauer. The other book is entitled *Jingles* and is dedicated to "Katherine from Mama." *Jingles* is a journal of Lute's poems many of which she refers to as sketches. The poetry dates from 1877 and includes the poetry in her alphabet books. Many of the poems deal with family and friends.

The first entry in *Jingles* is called "Life." Reflecting on the phases of life, the poem shows Lute's sensitivity to and appreciation for each life passage.

Life

1. *Baby-life's a bubble—laughing, cooing, crowing;*
   Not a care nor trouble; Doing naught but growing.

2. *Childlife is a story of the fairies' making.*
   Sunshine fills with glory all the hours of waking.

3. *Youthful-life's a romance; endless castles building,*
   Where the dreamy forms dance 'mid the fancied gilding.

---

* Author's Note: I have chosen to highlight the titles of family writings with italic.

4. *Middle-life's a history, sober facts involving;*
Often quite a mystery—Difficult in solving.

5. *Aged life's a waiting; thoughts and dreams all tending*
Toward the hope relating to the last—the ending.

L.L.B., as she so often signed her writings, also wrote a humorous short story about teenagers and mistaken identities. It's called "A Lark" and is really quite clever, but perhaps not as much as another story entitled "A Romance in Fourteen Letters." This is a story written in the form of letters between a mother and her daughter away at school. A favorite of mine, I believe it is autobiographical in some respects. You will find the story in the back of the book.

The Lute Bauer legacy I most treasure is *Toptown Toddlers*, a handmade book of poems, photographs and magnificent watercolors. "Rhymes and Snapshots by Lucy B. Bauer, Illustrated by Emma Sangston Spahr," this book is a rare treasure of a time long gone. Lute was not only a poet, but also a photographer! Her friend and fellow Club member Emma Spahr was a talented artist as well as seamstress.

The black-and-white snapshots which accompany each poem appear to have been posed, but they are quite clear today one hundred years after Lute and Emma collaborated on *Toptown Toddlers*. I have no trouble recognizing my great aunt Katherine Bauer in several snapshots and imagine the other children were cousins, neighbors, and the children of servants. The first poem sets the tone for the book and is entitled "Toptown Toddlers."

Way off in Toptown, on Tumblebed creek,
Such a quaint place, with its pure bracing air
I spent one summer, health's favor to seek,
One feels so rested, while sojourning there.

Studies of childhood are always a joy.
Toddlers in Toptown were friendly and rare,
And my good Kodak proved more than a toy,
Picturing childlife as I found it there.

Sketches I made of each wee boy and girl,
Snapshots I've taken will show you the more,
Surely you'll know them, if time's busy whirl
Takes you to Toptown, on Tumblebed's shore.

The black children described in Toptown would have been stereotypical versions of Negro servants who worked for the successful German American families of the city at the turn of the century. It was during this time that the fine houses of prosperous Germans began to dot the area from Tenth to Sixteenth and then move north beyond Sixteenth. The Schnull-Rauch house (today housing the Junior League of Indianapolis) is an elegant statement about its owner's success as were the expensive furnishings and many servants who waited on the family. "Your grandfather likes to be served," Mrs. Schnull told her grandchildren of a later generation.

Lute did not have an entourage, but like most of the prosperous women of the day, she had maids and a cook. Her black help were direct descendents of slaves. One maid told my grandmother Lucy stories of her early life in slavery. As I recall the story, she had been separated from her family. There was no slavery in Indiana; it was instead known for its underground railroad prior to and during the Civil War. In *Toptown Toddlers*, Lute photographed black children, probably the children of her maids, and wrote poems about their personalities. Her descriptions of these black children makes one uncomfortable and embarrassed now, a hundred years later. However, Lute couldn't even imagine a future with integration and civil rights. While some of the words and imagery in these poems are offensive to today's reader, I do not believe it was Lute's intention to be disrespectful. Her poems are a reflection of the culture and society of the late nineteenth century.

Chloe and Lizy Jane

Two small happy colored babies live in Toptown's little lane
They're my washerwoman's daughters, little Chloe and Lizy Jane;
They wear their hair in twists. They suck their chubby fists . . .

For when Mammy goes out washing, she leaves baby in her care
And the little Chloe will grin, And the fist goes farther in
As she turns her black eyes up to favor Lizy with a stare.

Lizy helps to wash the dishes, takes her broom and sweeps the
floor,
How could any little toddler help her mammy any more?
She says she's learning how to be housemaid to " de quality."

And she'll keep their houses shining with the duster and the
broom.
I am sure she'll look so bright, with her cap and apron white,
The big folks all will like to have her working in the room.

Lute's poem entitled "Ananias" reflects fully the racial attitudes of her class around 1898, but she probably meant the poem as a caring tribute to Ananias. With its bouncy meter, it's not hard to imagine a child in the 1890s skipping rope to the rhythm of "Ananias." In part, it goes:

Ananias

Small piccaninny—fat, black, and, grinny,
Bes' boy in Toptown his mammy would say,
Called Ananias, Daddy's so pious,
He found that name in the Bible one day . . .

Snapshots accompany Lute's poems of the children she described as did watercolor sketches of the children of Toptown. I hope they had fun posing for Lute and Emma Spahr, and I wonder if they ever saw the book and what happened to them in later years. Lute Bauer loved children and had marvelous powers of observation. I believe in this verse she wrote in the style of James Whitcomb Riley with some of the flavor of Booth Tarkington in *Penrod*.

Frances Celestine Branham died in 1899 after a long illness. Her funeral was held in the home of her eldest daughter, Mrs. George Bauer.

Edward Branham, Lute's father, died at the age of eighty-one in 1906. The story of his accidental death was reported in the papers. Edward Branham, pioneer jobber in shoes and "remarkably vigorous and youthful of spirit, was run down by an automobile at Illinois and Michigan Streets" suffering a fractured skull. [The history of the Branham and Taylor families is found in the Appendix.]

The following year, 1907, Lute Bauer, now fifty-five and having overseen her older daughter Lucy's wedding that spring to Hiram Raffensperger, accompanied daughter Katherine (who was twenty) to Europe. She wasn't the only German American from Indiana to go. Social columns of the newspapers of the day told of many such fashionable departures via steamship. German American families, well aware of how Bismark and the Kaiser had reunified the Fatherland and were making its name known in Europe, were taking a new pride in the home of their grandparents' birth. Many traveled abroad and Germany was a favorite destination.

Father George Bauer stayed home to represent his company, Ko-We-Ba Foods. The German American community he was a part of continued to thrive. The Indianapolis Maennerchor sang enthusiastically in the German tongue, and the club, founded by George's father, had expanded to include non-singing members. In 1907 the Maennerchor dedicated its new hall at Michigan and Illinois Streets. Charles W. Fairbanks, Vice-President of the United States and a Maennerchor member himself, spoke at the dedication. There were German newspapers in 1907 and German was taught in the public schools. Having hosted the national Turnfest, when gymnastic teams from all over the United States and Germany competed in Indianapolis, the city was chosen in 1907 as the new home of the Normal College of the American Gymnastic Union.

Two other clubs had joined the many which appealed to the gregarious German Americans. The "Portfolio" was composed of painters, sculptors, architects, and writers, and the "Lyra Casino," was primarily a society of musicians who performed private concerts of classical music. My husband's grandfather, Frank Maus Fauvre, was a member of the Athenaeum and the Lyra Casino, which included groups for whist-playing, dancing, singing and bowling. His favorite was the

bowling. Frank Fauvre was also a member of the "Indianapolis Schüt-
zenverein," a target shooting club. A frequent winner in the club, he
received prizes including several gold medals, a gold watch and innu-
merable turkeys at holiday time.

The Fauvres' first home was on north West Street, but in 1895 they
built a new residence at 28 west North Street between Meridian and
Illinois streets. A yellow brick house, it had limestone pillars at the
entrance, frescoed walls in the drawing and music rooms, tiled floor
and wainscot in the kitchen and both electric and gas light fixtures. It
was one of the first private residences in Indianapolis to be wired for
electricity and to have a telephone. While living on North Street, the
Fauvres hosted a dinner party for Governor and Mrs. Matthews. They
also held a large reception for William Jennings Bryan during his cam-
paign for the presidency of the United States in 1900.

Though the Bauers may not have traveled in all the same social
circles as other German American families of Indianapolis, their paths
undoubtedly crossed through these various organizations. Success was
theirs and a symbol of that success was to travel and study abroad. The
Fauvres traveled to Europe with their children in 1901 and again in
1910. Lute and Katherine Bauer, enjoying the success of George's
standing in the community, were proud to enjoy to the fullest their
opportunity to travel abroad, too. After traveling through Switzerland,
they settled in Berlin, where Katherine studied the violin with a German violinist named Arthur Hartmann. True to her nature, Lute wrote
long, descriptive letters of their experiences. Her sister, Kate Branham,
saved several of them. Lute wrote of their daily life, first in Geneva
and then in Berlin, from August through November of 1907. The letters make fascinating reading. An example follows:

Geneve, Suisse Aug. 11, 1907
  I was urged to go to church this morning, but refused, as I could do
more talking to my homefolks by staying at home. Kath stayed at home
because I did . . . We have been going a great deal lately, trying to see
everything and our time is growing short.
  Yesterday we took one of the steamers for a three hour's ride, and it
was great. Stopped at 5 towns. We also have been to the Kursaal—a

sort of amusement house. They have vaudeville here, but like the French theatre in the Parc des Eaux Vives—they have gambling devices, of all kinds in the big hall outside and they have two intermissions of 15 minutes each for the audience to go out and gamble. The French are natural gamblers, and besides that they have no modesty at all. I never saw the likes.

Why this evening we were sitting out in front of the Hotel Victoria, one of the principle hotels here, and a man, woman, boy & girl came along. When they got to the corner, the boy took short and the woman unbuttoned him and he relieved himself right facing us. I deserve great credit that I held my tongue.

I like Geneva for a short time but you couldn't hire me to live here. These deceitful French don't suit me, and they're so snippy looking. How they do ogle after Americans. I must tell you a coincidence. The other afternoon Mrs. Levy, Miss LeBarth, Vine, Kath and I were going to the park called the Jonction. We were walking quietly along and two young fellows came by in an automobile. They tipped their hats as they passed, and afterwards turned around and came back and invited us to take a ride. We of course paid no attention to them, and they went on, but were turning back to pass us again, when we quietly stepped into a cafe, and took some lemonade. We drew the curtains and they did not see us, as they passed back twice, and, I suppose didn't know where we were. We went in and out of sight mainly on account of Miss LeBarth, as she is a native of Geneva and was scared to death at them. Otherwise, I should have done like Rene's young friend on St. Clair Street and slapped their faces. But this goes to show you how very important it is for a young lady to be chaperoned in France.

Lute described in beautiful detail an excursion up the Grand Saleve mountain via cog train and donkey and expressed regret that the rest of her family and friends could not join her and Kath in experiencing the beauty of the Alps. She spoke of the open cafes and the fact the saloons were open on Sundays and half the night. She looked forward to having a rocking chair in Germany, as all the chairs in Switzerland seemed to be straight-backed.

Lute's hobby of photography had become an international favorite by the turn of the century, thanks to George Eastman's Kodak camera and the simplification of the developing process. She left her family a photographic history of her trip to Europe with Katherine. In her letter from Geneva she mentions taking pictures in front of the homes of John Calvin and the composer Franz Liszt, concluding with a few lines which showed how, despite her enjoyment of such an adventure, she really missed her family:

Sunny France is beautiful, but its people, and those of Switzerland, are not my kind. I tell you, I wonder how the real Swiss are. The Genevese all seem to be French . . . I am anxious to hear from all of you. I have heard once from Geo, twice from Lucy & twice from Mary, but I guess the rest of you will report before long. Kath joins me in love to everyone. I shall likely write my next from Berlin . . . Take care of George and Lucy. I am so anxious to hear how she enjoyed her trip. I do miss her so, no one knows. When I think of you all so far away, I just think of something else as quick as I can, so I won't dwell on the subject. Tell me all you do and how you are, and write often.

From Geneva, Lute and Kath traveled by train to Berlin, stopping briefly in Interlaken, Luzern and Frankfort. Seventy-one years after her great-grandfather Philip Sachs had left Germany, Katherine Bauer returned. Lute's next letter to her club friends described their trip and their adjustment to Berlin where Kath was to study:

Berlin Aug. 1907
As we passed through the country, we could almost feel and see ourselves leaving Switzerland and entering Germany. The style of architecture was so very different, and really we imagined a greater tone of thrift among the German farms and villages. I felt as if I had shaken treachery behind me, and entered in among an honest, industrious nation.

We saw magnificent homes and all the old churches, synagogues and cathedrals. We saw 3 elegant synagogues, there are 45,000 Jews in Frankfort . . .

[Finishing her description of visiting Goethe's home] *I stood
at the desk where he wrote, hoping some of the genius might rub off.
We were surprised and delighted with Frankfort and the old part of it
makes old Geneva look like a modern city.*

*I cannot describe Berlin. It is so big it takes my breath away. One
thing I am very sure of is that I don't want to be off in any part of the
city by myself—and I was too glad to get a chance to have apartments
right in Mrs. McElwee's neighborhood.*

*I find her house anything but stiff and uppish. It is a real home for
girls. I preferred my own quarters, however, and Mrs. McE. fixed the
price of one she had—until it came within my idea of what we should
spend. It will cost the same as some of the pensions we figured on first
and is quiet and furnished completely. We have a sitting room with 2
ROCKERS, and a bathroom, all furnished complete . . . This house has
an elevator that everyone works for himself. You unlock the door, unless the light is lit, which shows the elevator to be in use. Then you close
both doors after you and touch the button numbered like the floor you
want to stop at, and you go up and stop there. I never saw one before .
. ..*

*Katherine has concluded to study with Hartmann. He seems to be
the big one here. We have met him, and he is not at all scary. We were
both favorably impressed with him. She hasn't played for him yet, but
will go to see him in the near future.*

*After a supper party, eight of us attended the Royal Opera to hear
Traviata. We had elegant seats for 75 cts. I was relieved to find that
they do not dress for opera—unless the Emperor is to be present. The
Royal box is the only one in the house and over all the people's heads.
The opera was fine—and Frances thought it a great thing that the first
opera we attended in Berlin should have for its star an American girl,
born in Indianapolis. She is a Miss Marcia Craft, about 26 years old—
and she surely took the people by storm. She was called before the cur-
tain over a dozen times, and everyone is raving over her.*

*. . . Tell Maze I wish I could send over one of these native nurses
[nuns with enormous white winged headdresses] in a letter—for Edward—they are sights to behold—They look like a cross between a wind-
mill and a turkey gobbler in full sail. I'm going to take a snapshot of one*

of them, and send home. They are curiosities, but some of them are very pretty faced girls indeed.

Berlin, August 26, 1907

We are, of course, delighted with the affairs, as they have shaped themselves. The McElwees and the whole household are very enthusiastic about Kath's playing and I go a great deal upon the opinion of such people, who are hand in glove with such artists as stand highest in Europe. Let us hope that the kid will equal their expectations and Lucy will think herself an oracle when she thinks of the side remark she has often made to me—"Mama, there's no use talking; the kid gets a different quality of tone from the rest of them." Last night she played Nimiawski's Romance, in the Music Salon—and afterward Traumerei. They all wanted to know where on earth she got so much soul—at such an age. Then afterwards we had quite a red letter evening. First Arthur Hartmann came, and afterward Arthur Nevin, the composer. We talked a while and then Nevin sat at the piano and gave us explanations and played his entire new Indian opera which is to be brought out in Dresden this winter. He spent summers among the Indians getting their war songs, love songs, lullabies and chants. He was sent by a company for that purpose, and afterwards told why . . . This opera is based on a legend of the Black Foot Indians.

Afterwards Frances made welsh rabbit in the dining room and served that and beer. As we are on the water wagon, we partook freely of the rabbit but passed by the beer. We went to bed at 12 o'clock and this morning did not waken until after 9. I accused Frances of putting dope in the rabbit but she denied it. At any rate this climate makes a fellow sleep sound. Gee! there's the sun! This is Kath's first lesson day, 5 o'clock this evening. She is feeling grunty, which is too bad. I have her covered up on the couch to keep warm and hope the pains stay away.

On learning that a teacher preparing for her American tour had collected a magnificent wardrobe including pink lace crepe de chine underclothes, Lute said it

. . . makes me firm that I shall never go to stay with Mme. Gadski

all night—for she might not take to my gauze union suits and Wasson's [an Indianapolis department store] nightgowns. Rats! She hasn't any two girls like mine, and she hasn't Geo Bauer and she hasn't the club either so she can go hang with her pink panties.

Repeatedly justifying her decision to have their own apartment near the McElwee rooming house and how pleased she was of the arrangement and her role as chaperone, Lute also wrote of their visit to the Hohm Zollern Museum. There she found fault in the stitching she found on some of the displayed costumes. She goes on to say:

I am certain I have done right, and he (Geo) must be content knowing we will not risk anything. Living here and everything else is expensive enough, goodness knows, but we can live well on $65 a month or less and I know we could not board half way for that . . . I want to live as economically as I can, not to stint ourselves on our eats. That I will not do. Washing is reasonable and beautifully done. Car fare is 2 $1/2$ cts. Cab fare (or rather droschkes, as they call them, they are all open phaetonlike things) is never over 30 cts. for the two of us to go to the other end of town. You can't understand these things unless you see them. Music lessons are high, but that's what we expected. Hartmann's prices are $7.50 a lesson, but Miss Patton says sometimes the lessons are 2 hours long. I shall always be with Katharine, no matter where she is. We can have one best dress apiece and not have to wear it at home.

Mrs. McElwee says that the women here wear the same dress to all the receptions and teas and everywhere—that they do not need variety like at home, and dress is not considered, so long as you look clean and in order.

Kath was so completely disgusted with the American girls of Geneva who fell in with the disgusting ways of the country that there would never be any danger of her doing likewise. Mr. Hartmann said I would be very welcome to come to the lessons, just as I always have done—so there is no change of our usual arrangements.

I was particularly fond of the collection of Queen Louise. What a beautiful woman she was, and yet she had to always throw a light scarf across the front of her throat to hide a goiter. Now I haven't anything to hide except my stomach —so I'm better off.

At the end of this letter, Lute shares her wish that family and friends could afford to visit her and Katherine in Berlin. She wrote, "Oh, if Carnegie would only furnish the money, instead of sticking libraries everywhere!"

A week later she wrote her brother and sisters of having the exciting opportunity to experience the pomp and circumstance of the Kaiser reviewing the troops. In 1907 the Kaiser was at his height of impressiveness. Those of German American heritage were filled with pride at his strong German nationalism, as the emperor of the Germans sought colonies and built a navy so Germans would stand "foremost among European nations." Soon their pride would turn to bewilderment and sadness.

Lute and Katherine were also privileged to be asked to attend the opera with Berlin society, but Lute, the modest Midwestern American, refused to accept the challenge of the appropriate dress code. Lute was not about to expose her ample bosom!

Berlin Sept. 2, 1907

I have seen the Kaiser—and Kaiserin and they look just like a man and woman. I saw the Crown Prince and Princess. Also the King of Siam who didn't look like a man. I saw the Embassaries from Abysinnia, Japan, China and our own U.S. The other nations all looked alike. This morning we went to view one of the big events of Berlin: the review of the 60,000 men of the German army before the Kaiser. I never saw a grander sight in my life. It was held on Templehofer field, an immense clearing. There were a dozen large grandstands and we were very lucky in getting places, for the Kaiser stood right before us—the Crown Prince by his side—both on horseback, the Kaiserin and the Crown Princess in a carriage near them. Bands playing—and the men in perfect marching order.

We ate breakfast at 7 o'clock in order to get there. Some Americans sat behind us and they had the finest field glass I ever looked through, which they kindly shared with us. Some of the lazy folks in the house, who wouldn't get up so early will be sorry they missed such a sight. They are counting on seeing the royal family tonight at the opera when the women are obliged to wear decollette. This bars me out. If they had said I had to ride in on a billy goat I might have tried it, but turn out my anatomy for inspection? Not for me! I wanted Kath to go as her dresses were all right, but she wouldn't go where I couldn't. The Texas contingent of the household all ripped out their lace yokes for the occasion and Friday night when I went downstairs they were all trying on their clothes, and as I wrote Lucy the hall was full of skin and bones getting ready for Billy's party. We had real good fun over it and I told them I'd stay home and mix mustard to put on them when they returned so as to ward off pneumonia. These occasions only occur September & June but the royal family attend the opera very often and do not give notice on other occasions. Ladies dress like they were respectable . . .

I know Berlin stoves would be a curiosity to you all. I took a picture of the one in my room so as to show you all. I have not developed the films yet for I want to be undisturbed when I do and will wait until I am settled.

I like the all the girls in this house except one. She is too much for me to stomach but she's going home Wednesday or Thursday, I am happy to state. She is a Miss McFarland of Texas. She is about 4' 6" and a very pretty dollfaced girl of 19. If she only had some sense, but she comes the baby act and drawls out baby talk from morning till night—and I've heard so much about "My littel sef— my littel gown—my littel coat— and all my littel belongings" that I feel like drowning her. She says she's everybody's pet and I can tell her she isn't mine by a darned sight. If I had a girl like that, I couldn't look people in the face. Her maiden aunt is with her and waits on her like she was a superior being—carries her breakfast to her bed—and that sort of squash. I bet if Lucy was here, I'd have to muzzle her when this girl came around or she'd tell her a few facts about herself. You ought to see her freeze to anything with breeches on and coo around him. Let's thank our stars there is not a single fool among our girls . . .

Berlin Sept. 10th 1907 — 38 Motz Strasse
It seems funny not to have any dust on the furniture. Everything is

kept so clean on the streets and no place for dust to gather. This morning I went through the motions of dusting the rooms, but it wasn't at all necessary. I bought some toilet paper this afternoon. I wandered around until I saw some displayed on a counter, and then the rest was easy. If I hadn't run across it I would have come home without it, for my gift of pantomime wouldn't have done me any good unless I ran the risk of being arrested for indecency.

Though I suspect George Bauer could speak German well, obviously his very American wife could not. Kate Branham kept six of Lute's letters from Europe. In the last one dated November 20, Lute talks about the current fares for ocean voyages: $55 to $108, according to the time of year. She was delighted to find some American canned goods, even Van Camp's baked pork and beans, but was quick to tell the grocer that the very best brand of canned goods was Ko-We-Ba. She didn't buy the canned goods though—they were too expensive!

In one letter, Lute joked about her weight and apparently thinning hair: "I am greasing my head to keep my hair. The other night I saw a man without a spear on his head. He looked like a new born rat. I told Kath I felt like a buffalo at the side of him." When Lucy, her older daughter and my grandmother, grew older she often wore a small hairpiece on the back of her head to disguise her own thinning hair.

Lute Bauer and Kath returned to Indianapolis, but Lute was destined for more travel. In the spring of 1913, she and George went to California. George was in poor health. Lute's niece, Alice Branham Bradley, received two letters from her aunt written on Japanese stationery, tall, slender decorated sheets as thin as tissue paper.

Coronado, Cal.— Feb. 17, 1913

[George] *takes 2 1/2 qts. of milk a day, divided up in half hourly installments, and he is gradually dropping the medicine. Edward [their grandchild and my uncle] wanted to know if Andad took his milk from a bottle. I wrote back that the bottles were brought in to his bed, but he took his milk from a glass thro' a straw.*

I saw a bird man in a hydroplane this morning. They fly down here over the bay, every day, but are always a wonderful sight to me. I bet I come home fat as a pig, for I do eat so here. We have everything in the fashion of the Battle Creek food [cereals like shredded wheat], and no meat to speak of—Have had fish and chicken. I'm going to make a vegetarian out of Uncle George. He says when he gets to eating he don't intend to do much meat eating.

We had a couple of earthquake shocks the other night. They were not serious, but had we been in San Francisco, I should have gotten out by first train. They do not have hard ones here, but it was quite enough for us. We are only a short distance from the big Coronado Hotel and I go up there occasionally, just to watch everyone pose for everyone else. It's all an empty sham, this high society stunt, and they can have it. I'm always glad to get back here to real life.

In those days the Coronado Hotel, which still dominates Coronado Island, had a health spa. Elaborate tents were erected on the grounds and the guests, who stayed in them were pampered. Undoubtedly, the Coronado facilities were much more expensive than those chosen by the Bauers.

Coronado — April 20th, 1913

I went out to the Country Club to lunch yesterday with Mrs. Geo Barney and had a dandy time . . . then we went in San Diego to see the little bungalow used as a showroom for disappearing beds. It has six rooms and one is a kitchen. The other five contain 14 beds, and you can't find one of them. They shoot out from hat racks, divans, desks, dressers, doors, buffets and panels, and when you get sleepy, all you have to do is stand where you are and tumble in. I have a lot of literature on the subject, and will show you the illustrations when I come to club.

I enclose a clipping from last night's paper of the old Chinese boat that lies in the harbor here. It is a curiosity, and is full of instruments of torture used in the old days. When I cross the harbor on the ferry, I always gaze in wonder at it, as something that is actually older than I am.

When Lute wrote her family from Coronado, she was a grandmother. My Uncle Ed, first child of their daughter Lucy, was four years old when his maternal grandparents traveled to the West Coast. They stayed on Coronado from February through April, 1913. Two months after their return to Indianapolis, they greeted another grandson, George William Raffensperger, my father.

Lucy's sister Katherine (Tattie) had not yet found a husband in the spring of 1913, but she was soon to find one. I'm not sure how or where Tattie met her future husband, Clarke Allin, a Canadian by birth, but they must not have known each other long when he proposed marriage. They were married in 1914.

Lute and George Bauer returned to Coronado in the spring of 1915. Lute was sixty-three and George fifty-nine. On March 21, 1915, Lute wrote her sisters on health spa stationery. The letterhead reads HALSOHEM (Up-To-Date Methods of Effective Nature Healing) 624-634 Glorietta Blvd. Coronado. She wrote

I have just finished a letter to the children, and want to write to you and our club before I stop. This is a beautiful sunny day—almost too hot. George is out basking in the sun like an alligator, and comes in every half hour to drink some milk. We ate some truck [produce, I assume] in San Diego that didn't taste good, so he has had a little squeamishness in his stomach as a result and Dr. Berggren put him on orange juice for the past 3 days, and now on milk for a day or two, so as to get him in good shape for the rest of our trip.

He and I went over with Elwarners last night to see Crane in David Harum at a movie. It was real good. After we got home, we played cards awhile, and then read after we got in bed, until we got sleepy.

We enjoyed San Diego and the Exposition, but it is lovely to be over here. Everything is blooming and beautiful, and everyone so pleasant. The air is so clear this morning that we can see the big table mountain of Mexico quite clearly. It is 90 miles away in Mexico and looks just behind the mountains of San Diego. George seems in good spirits.

The Exposition here is beautiful, as to buildings and landscape gardening. It could not be improved on. But we were disappointed in the exhibits which were no doubt curtailed on acct. of the war. Japan and

Mexico I believe are the only foreign exhibits. They say there is much more in San Francisco, but their Expo. is not nearly so beautiful as this one.

I must close now and leave a place for Geo to write a few lines. He enjoyed his birthday outfit so much, and immediately sat down and wrote 20 letters and cards with his new fountain pen, and has worn his sleeve buttons ever since, and they are surely beauties.

Love to all friends —and lots of it for yourselves. Write when you can.

Lute left a space at the end of her letter for George. He added the following lines, but not with his new fountain pen. He wrote in pencil in handwriting so shaky as to be barely legible:

Am OK, but would like to see you all—Lute has written about everything. If Katherine goes to Noblesville while Hiram is away from home, make some arrangements for one of you or Kate or Rene to stay with her [Lucy] nights.

With lots of love, Geo"

It's hard to imagine what San Diego and San Francisco were like in 1915, without today's population. It is interesting to know that my great-grandparents liked my adopted state and spent much time in California. As to George's health, I can only guess that perhaps an ulcer or heart disease brought him to a European style health spa. According to the San Diego Historical Society, health spas were most popular in the teens. Halsohem is a Swedish word meaning health and home. The spa was in operation until 1919. The building was torn down in the past twenty years and a modern home has taken its place.

In October of that year, 1915, Lute and George suffered probably the greatest loss of their lives. Daughter Katherine died only a few months after their return from San Diego.

Katherine Bauer Allin
(1889–1915)

Thanks to the many reminiscences of my grandmother, I grew up feeling I knew my great-aunt, the concert violinist. She had been the pride of her family and beloved by all. As a third grader in the Indianapolis Public School system, I was given the opportunity to take violin lessons. My grandmother gave me Katherine's first violin to use, and I suspect expectations were high that I just might have her talent for the instrument. I did not. In fact, I found the violin the most incredibly complex and perplexing musical instrument!

Katherine filled her short life with music. She enriched the lives of all who heard her play and was beloved by her family and friends. As a child, she had shown marked talent and after receiving her first lessons from her relative, Nannie Branham, she studied with Hugh McGibney until she graduated from Manual Training High School. In Berlin, Germany, she studied with eminent violinist Arthur Hartmann. Her playing was reported to be "refined, full of musicality and characterized by a maturity usually obtained only by a person many years her senior."

Though it wouldn't be long before World War I subdued the enthusiastic German American community, Lute and her daughter chose to cling to their memories of Germany and honor its cultural emphasis by founding a German Indianapolis musical club. *The Indianapolis News* of February 22, 1914 reported

> *Indianapolis and the Hoosier custom of formal entertaining seem far away indeed at the meetings on Sunday afternoons of the Berlin Club, a local organization that is decidedly novel.*
>
> *The club, as its name implies, is composed entirely of Indianapolis women who have lived in Berlin and the idea of the organization originated when a group of Indianapolis musicians were in that city in the*

winter of 1908 pursuing their studies, among them being Miss Bertha and Miss Pauline Schellschmidt and their sister, Mrs. William Koehne, then Miss Louise Schellschmidt, as well as Miss Katherine Bauer, the violinist, and her mother, Mrs. George Bauer.

These Indianapolis folk, with a number of others who came and went during that year, often met at Sunday afternoon concerts and musicals and, of course, the conversation frequently drifted to Hoosier land, with plans for the future at home. Many times there were suggestions that the joy of those Sunday afternoon musicals might be continued "at home."

Many of the delightful features of the German musicals are retained and the gatherings always are purely informal, with that fascinating atmosphere that characterizes the continental Sunday afternoon entertaining.

By the time of her marriage to Clarke Allin at twenty-five, Katherine had already won a wide reputation as a violinist. The Berlin Club concerts provided her an opportunity to share her talents, and her work always filled in a great part of the classics programs in the club. The club changed its name to the Matinee Musicale, because of anti-German sentiment during the early days of World War I. *The Indianapolis News* reported in both Katherine's and Lute's obituaries that they had been members of the Matinee Musicale, but there is no further mention of the Berlin Club.

The German American community, was, of course, anguished at the coming of the Great War. At first they defended the Fatherland and begged Americans to withhold judgment in the European struggle. Charles Mayer, John Frenzel, Herman Lieber and others in Indianapolis signed a letter at the beginning of the war explaining and defending the German position. Described as prominent Germans, whose loyalty to America could not be questioned, their letter was read on the floor of the House of Representatives. Still, as the war progressed and America eventually entered, the German contingent in Indianapolis was torn. Finally loyalties were clarified; inevitably they supported America. To help avoid misunderstanding, the Maennerchor was temporarily renamed the "Academy of Music" and Das Deutsche

Haus became the "Athenaeum." Shubrick Kothe, nephew of William Kothe, has reported name-calling and public scorn of Germans suffered by his friends and relatives.

Cousin Kurt Vonnegut, Jr. wrote: "You remind me yet again that I myself was raised, because of my father's sensitivity to American hatred for Germans during World War One, without any celebration of or even information about German culture. Father said very little about the family past, but recalled again and again a hate letter he received during the War to End Wars which said, 'Stop teaching your God damn kids Dutch.' "

Indianapolis, however, stayed calm during the period; there were no anti-German demonstrations as in other cities.

By the end of World War I in Indianapolis German American families had become simply American. A decline in the German activities and organizations followed. German was no longer taught in the schools and the majority of the German-language newspapers went out of business. However, German traditions persisted into the generation of my father and his brother.

Many German families in Indianapolis intermarried: Vonneguts married Liebers, Kothes married Liebers. Large homes and entourages of servants continued as custom. It was during this time that the famous Schnull-Rauch New Year's Eve parties began, to continue as elegant social events for the still strong German American families in the community. Shubrick Kothe recalls his parents attending the Schnull parties held in the ballroom on the third floor of their home in the twenties. He described these society parties he and Mrs. Kothe later attended in the forties as formal events where the men wore tails and the women long gowns. After going through a receiving line, guests were treated to a purple-colored German punch, champagne and a bountiful buffet table of German dishes. Entertainment included a German ensemble band and dancing. The waltz was popular. Midway through the evening some of the male guests would gather and sing the old German songs. He recalls that besides the Kothes, guests included the Kuhns, Frenzels, Hitzes, and Metzgers. The Bauers may have attended the early Schnull soirees, but if they did I never heard about it. However, it would be no surprise if the Frank Maus Fauvres did attend, since their eldest son, Francis, married Bertha Schnull.

It was during this period that Tattie was enjoying her new marriage to Clarke Allin. In September of 1915, however, Tattie developed appendicitis and was hospitalized. Three weeks later, she died of complications. She was twenty-six years old, still a bride of barely a year.

Despite the brevity of their marriage, Clarke Allin was warmly received into the Bauer family and lived with them for a while. As long as he was in Indiana, he joined them at family Christmases and get-togethers. There are many pictures of "Doc," as the family called him, in the photo albums. He was a man with a wonderful sense of humor. I recall my grandmother crying when he died right before Christmas, 1949. He had moved back to Canada, I believe, but they had kept in touch. To my knowledge Clarke never remarried. He is buried next to his wife of a year, Katherine.

Tattie's death devastated the Bauer family. The grief experienced by George Bauer, her father, may have even hastened his own death, for he died only three years later.

George Bauer
(1856-1918)

My great-grandfather George Bauer had a stiff, gruff manner which tended to intimidate people, but not his wife Lute. Like many German men of his time, George was probably autocratic, but his wife's sense of humor and liberated spirit kept him in line. She must have understood George the businessman as being intense and ambitious. And I suspect that she also understood that he had long been the "man of the family" since losing his father at such a young age.

George, however, had a kind heart. When it was discovered that Lute's niece, Edith, was unable to nurse her daughter because her milk was poisoning the baby, George came to the rescue. Through his sources at Ko-We-Ba, he found a suitable canned formula that saved the child's life.

For seventeen years George Bauer traveled the Midwest representing the interests of his company, Ko-We-Ba foods. In 1907, however, he became the treasurer and buyer for Kothe, Wells & Bauer, after the company's incorporation. This probably enabled him to spend more time at home with his wife and daughters. Eventually, however, hard work hastened George's demise. *The Indianapolis News* reported

> *Mr. Bauer, accompanied by his wife, departed last week for California in the hope of improving his health. He had been suffering from a complication of diseases caused by overwork. The telegram yesterday said Mr. Bauer was stricken with a heart attack as his train neared Colton and died before medical aid could be secured.*

Lute was with George at the time of his death. They had enjoyed thirty-eight years of marriage. Following his death, the secretary of his company sent Lute a copy of a resolution passed by the Board of Directors of Kothe, Wells & Bauer. It read in part

The death of Mr. George Bauer our Treasurer, and one of the founders of our business, is a great loss to us in the conduct of the business and as a member of the Board of Directors. His great ability, untiring energy and devotion to his duties, his never-failing courtesy and his absolute unselfishness, endeared him to everyone associated with him . . .

Mr. George Bauer was a man among men in every way, whether in business or in a personal way and we, the Directors of the Kothe, Wells, & Bauer Company, pay this tribute to his memory.

On Christmas Day following his death, Lute wrote an inspirational quote for her daughter:

To Lucy B. Raffensperger with love from Mama — Dec. 25th, 1919

No grief can be so great as to shatter a whole life.
Every sorrow, even every sin, comes to us with a special message; not to deaden, but to quicken us.
Suffer to the utmost, if need be, but never be overcome.
Be calm, as one who believes in God, should be.
Step firm, tho' you walk over burning coals.

Lucy framed this quote. I remember it sitting on my grandmother's dresser. After her death, it was given to me by my father. One day, wondering if there might be a photograph hiding behind the affirmation, I removed the backing of the little 5 by 7-inch tarnished frame and found instead a message from my grandmother, Lucy Bauer Raffensperger. On September 12, 1949, she had written

This is a quotation which has been handed down in my family for over 100 years. Mama wrote this page in a [New] Testament which she gave me several years before her death and since it is becoming yellow and worn, I am trying to preserve it. The book is in shreds. It has helped me as it has countless others in despair so treasure it and hand it on. Love, Mother.

Lucy Raffensperger, the daughter of Lute Bauer and "Babboo" to me, gave me a New Testament and Psalms on her son's thirtieth birthday. At the time my father was serving in the Navy in the South Pacific and I was three. I think she feared that I might lose my father in the war. On the inside of the front flyleaf Lucy quoted the inspirational message her mother had passed on to her and at the end she added: *From a Branham family diary of 1810, handed down* [over the years in] *several diaries.* A year after writing that message for her daughter, Lute died. Perhaps she knew her time was near and anticipated the grief her daughter Lucy would experience because, true to her nature, she had used words to try to ease the pain.

Lucy (Lute) Bushrod Branham Bauer died in Indianapolis July 17, 1920. Her obituary was printed the very day of her death by *The Indianapolis News*. She outlived her husband by only two years and died at home in the three story house she and her husband had shared with their daughter and her family at 4240 Washington Boulevard. By all standards, Lute lived a very full and interesting life. In addition to being a founding member of the "Long Thread Needle Club" and the Indianapolis Matinee Musicale, she was a prolific writer whose works expressed the creative talents of her generation and have provided subsequent generations much pleasure.

THE STATE OF INDIANA, MARION COUNTY, SCT:

TO ALL TO WHOM THESE PRESENTS SHALL COME--GREETING:

Know ye, That at the _April_ Term, in the year eighteen hundred and fifty _Six_ of the _Marion Circuit_ Court of the County of Marion aforesaid, _John George Bauer_ made the proof and took the oath to support the Constitution of the United States, and the oath of Allegiance required by law, before said Court, and was then, that is to say, on the _Third_ day of _July_ 1856 by said Court, duly admitted a Citizen of the United States.

In witness of which, I, William Stewart, Clerk of said Court, hereunto affix the Seal thereof, and subscribe my name, at Indianapolis, this _3-d_ day of _July_, 185 6.

Court Clerk

John George Bauer's 1850 citizenship papers, proudly saved by his family.

Mary Sachs Bauer as a young woman and wife of George Bauer.

George Bauer, merchant tailor and "Forty-eighter."

"Social Turngemeinde," the first Turner (Gymnastic) Hall in Indianapolis located at 117 N. Noble Street in 1852. A new site was acquired at Kentucky and Tennessee (Capitol) Avenues in 1854, four years before the death of George Bauer, one of its members.

Maennerchor Hall, 337 E. Washington Street, 1878.

The German-English Independent School 230 E. Maryland Street, 1867.

Mary Bauer, George's sister.

George Bauer, Jr., as a young man and wholesale grocer.

Elizabeth Bauer, George's sister.

Aunt Liz at age eighty and still working.

Lute Bauer's "Long Thread Needle Club" about which she wrote a history in 1914. The charter members were Mrs. J. O. Spahr, Mrs. John H. Spahr, Miss Mary Spahr, Mrs. C. A. Bookwalter, Mrs. A. M. Glossbrenner, Mrs. W. Speer, Mrs. W. J. Riley, Mrs. A. C. Daily, Mrs. Rena Kittle, and Mrs. George Bauer. This gathering was photographed at the Bookwalter home.

A photo of one of the city's turn-of-the century black children became the basis for "Ananias," a watercolor sketch in Lute's *Top Town Toddlers*.

The commercial district on South Meridian Street as seen from Monument Circle in the 1890s. Ko-We-Ba Foods located in this district.

Lute Bauer was a photographer as well as poet. These photos were taken during 1907 when she accompanied daughter Katherine (Tattie) to Europe. Tattie may have excelled as a young violinist, but the romantic wardrobe and the size of her waist are also worth noting!

In 1887 Lute Bauer made alphabet books for daughter Lucy Mary, age three, and her Taylor cousins, Nancy and Rene Ohr. Almost identical, the books are illustrated with colorful cutouts and sketches. Lute's poems often included the names of her daughter's playmates, like the children of William Kothe.

Lucy Mary Bauer at the time of her graduation from Manual Training High School, 1903. She had already attracted the attention of Hiram Raffensperger, a fellow classmate.

The interior of Charles Mayer & Co. around 1900.

George Bauer, Jr., and the women of his family with Lucy's little son Ed and nanny.

Lute Bauer and her two talented daughters, Lucy Mary and Katherine (Tattie).

Christmas, 1910, with little Ed Raffensperger and the tree.

Ko-We-Ba ads in *The Indianapolis Trade Journal,* including one showing the building.

60

Lucy Raffensperger and little Ed.

Grandmother Lute with her first grandchild, H. Edward Raffensperger.

4240 Washington Boulevard, the three-story Bavarian style home built by the Bauers and the Raffenspergers.

Lucy Raffensperger with Ed and baby brother, Bill, in 1913.

The

Raffenspergers

The Raffenspergers

Christian Raffensperger (date unknown) *m*. Catherine —— (date unknown)

Philip Haverstock (1749) *m*. Barbara Breber (1754)

Martin Raffensperger (1790) *m*. Dorothea Haverstock (1794)

Hiram Chance (date unknown)

Martin Raffensperger, Jr. (1815) *m*. Amanda Chance (1838)

Joseph Losier (1830) *m*. Margarete Anna —— (1832)
3 children: John Joseph, Anna & Sophie Losier

Margarete Losier *m*. Herman W. Schowe
5 children including Sophie Schowe (1865)

Hiram Clinton Raffensperger (1857) *m*. Anna Losier (1859)
3 sons: Burton, Hiram Joseph and Arthur Clinton

Charles Duty Howell (1888) *m*. Katherine Ann Shockley (1889)
1 daughter: Eunice Mae

Hiram Joseph Raffensperger (1884) *m*. Lucy Mary Bauer (1884)
2 sons: Ed and Bill

George William Raffensperger (1913) *m*. Eunice Mae Howell (1915)
1 daughter: Beverly

Hiram Edward Raffensperger (1909) *m*. Alberta Alexander (1909)
no children

Caspar Maus (1816) *m*. Magdalena Dietriche (1819)
11 children

Frank M. Fauvre (1851) *m*. Lillian Scholl (1859)
7 children

Irving M. Fauvre (1895) *m*. Mildred Lorraine Van Allen Clizbe (1905)
2 sons: Charles Clizbe and David Van Allen

David Van Allen Fauvre (1938) *m*. Beverly Howell Raffensperger (1939)
2 children: David William and Cynthia Elise

The Raffensperger Roots

Perhaps the most frustrating thing about having a long, uncommon name is that it is so often misspelled as well as mispronounced. The historical documents and letters my grandfather, Hiram Joseph Raffensperger, saved from his own ancestral research show such misspellings as Raffensberger, Raffensburger, even Rafflesberger! It is possible that the name may have originally been Rauschenburger—but *Raffensperger* was my family's name.

The Raffenspergers were Pennsylvania Dutch who settled in York County, Pennsylvania, in the eighteenth century. The Pennsylvania Dutch (which is a misinterpretation of the word *Deutsch*, meaning German) were people from the German Rhineland. Some came from the German part of Switzerland; others were Huguenots, French Protestants. In search of religious freedom, these Germans came to William Penn's colony, which was geographically reminiscent of home. Settling primarily in eastern Pennsylvania, they made up half the population of the colony by 1750. The Pennsylvania Germans were mostly of the Lutheran or Reformed Churches and referred to as "the church people." Some groups included the Amish and Mennonite, known later as "the plain people" because of their simple dress and distrust of formal church traditions.

Hiram Raffensperger traced his ancestry to Phillip Haverstock, a Revolutionary soldier who served as a member of the York County, Pennsylvania Militia, 7th Class, 3rd Company, 5th Battalion. Phillip Haverstock was born in 1749 in Pennsylvania. He married Barbara Breber, who was also born in Pennsylvania in 1754. Their daughter, Dorthea Haverstock, was born in York County in 1794 and married Martin Raffensperger, born 1790. Martin Raffensperger was the son of Christian and Catherine Raffensperger. Both Christian and his son Martin were members of the 7th Company, Fifth Battalion, York County Militia.

In 1958 Hiram and Lucy Raffensperger traveled to York, Pennsylvania, and found the gravestones of Christian and Martin Raffensperger, which they photographed. In their papers I found a program from a church service they probably attended in York. The Old Paradise Holtzschwamm Union Church is pictured on the program, which shows an adjacent Lutheran cemetery where I believe there are several Raffensperger tombstones.

Martin Raffensperger died in New Salem, Pennsylvania, in 1822, leaving a son who bore his name. Martin, Jr., was born in York County in 1815. His second wife was Amanda Chance, who was born in 1838 in North Codorus, York County.

Martin and Amanda married in Pennsylvania in 1855. Martin was forty-five and Amanda, twenty-two. I have a photograph of a man named Hiram Chance who was either Amanda's father or brother. The photo is not dated but shows a handsome, dark-bearded man in his thirties standing next to an elaborately carved straight-back chair. His clothes look baggy and rumpled. Martin and Amanda's son, Hiram Clinton Raffensperger, was born in York County in 1857 right before the Civil War. He was my great-grandfather.

Two years after Hiram Clinton's birth, his father, Martin Raffensperger, Jr., died in New Salem, Pennsylvania. Amanda moved her family to Indiana during or after the Civil War. Though not among the earliest German settlers in Indianapolis, the Raffenspergers contributed to the already-thriving German community.

Hiram Clinton Raffensperger
(1857–1909)

H. C. Raffensperger was a druggist in Indianapolis at the turn of the century. I have two photographs of his store, which was located on the southwest corner of East and South Streets. The photo of the exterior shows a modest establishment in a long, narrow brick building with what looks like an apartment above the drugstore. Beneath the curtained windows of the apartment one can see the name H. C. RAFFENSPERGER painted on a wood molding across the front of the building. On the side of the second story the word DRUGS is painted directly on the brick. Beneath this ad is another advertisement: "Ice-Cream-Soda—5 ct." The interior photo is more attractive, showing a long room of fully-stocked glass cases, garlanded gas chandeliers, wire and wood ice cream parlor chairs, and small round tables.

Indianapolis Illustrated said in rather florid prose:

> *One of the most popular druggists in the section of the city in which he is located is Mr. H. C. Raffensperger, who for the past seven years has been conducting a splendid, flourishing business at the southwest corner of East and South streets. A conspicuous feature of Mr. Raffensperger's popular pharmacy is a superb soda fountain from which delicious soda with pure fruit syrups is drawn.*
>
> *Mr. Raffensperger has had an experience compounding and dispensing medicines extending over a period of twenty-five years, and is fully acquainted with properties and values of drugs and medicines.*
>
> *The prescription laboratory is provided with all the modern adjuncts of utility and convenience to insure accuracy and promptitude, and physicians' orders are prepared and medicines dispensed at all hours by competent assistants.*
>
> *Mr. Raffensperger has resided in Indianapolis for some time, since early youth. He is a courteous gentleman, very popular in professional*

and social circles. He is a prominent member of the Marion County Drug Association, a director of the Plymouth Building and Loan Association, a 32nd degree Mason, Mystic Shrine, also of the Knights Templar and the K.of P.

Hiram Clinton, who apparently was also called Harvey according to some references, married Anna Losier on March 18, 1880, in Indianapolis. They had three sons: Arthur, Burt, and Hiram. Hiram Joseph, my grandfather, was born in Indianapolis in 1884.

I don't recall my grandfather talking very much about his father Hiram, but it must have been fun for him to have had access to that soda fountain as a young man. I know little of my great-grandmother, Anna Losier Raffensperger, or her influence on my grandfather. However, when I went through my grandfather's papers, I ran across a letter from an Aunt Sophie Schowe Wedge, Anna's half-sister, written shortly after Anna's death:

Oneco, Fla. – March 26, 1939

Dear Hiram & Lucy
Received your letter & certainly was pleased to hear from you. I am sending you a copie of the records I copied from Mother's german bible, and I found this clipping in her bible and I am sending it to you to read it about your uncle Joseph when he was elected postmaster in Jackson, Tenn. Mother was very proud of him.
It is rather sad that such a feeling existed in the family I never could understand it. Hiram's mother [Anna Losier] was a very good woman but she was very odd at times our family was poor and being poor is no disgrace, she didn't want anybody to know that we were poor and often didn't seem to want us to come to her house because we couldn't dress in style Mother often felt very bad about it but I never let it bother me I went to see her when ever I could. I was to see her 2 years ago, and I told her then to cast all ill feeling behind her & have more love for all that were near and dear to her. I know she was unhappy couldent help but be, but she had a spirit that wasent just what she ought to tolerate and she would have to pray for God to forgive her.

I am sorry you dident come to see us when you were so close to us, we sure would be glad to have you then we could talk things over. If there is anything more Hiram would like to know I will be glad to write more.

I imagine my grandparents contacted Sophie in an effort to learn more about Anna Losier Raffensperger, whose husband Hiram Clinton died at age fifty-two, leaving his wife of twenty-nine years and three sons. Sophie's letter included her translation of the family record kept in a German Bible. It has been most helpful in researching my grandfather's ancestry.

Joseph Losier was born in Watwell, St. Gallen, Switzerland, November 1830. He married Margarete Anna Losier, who was also born in St. Gallen, October 15, 1832. St. Gallen is in the northeastern part of Switzerland just south of Lake Constantine. The couple emigrated to the United States in the 1850s. Their firstborn, Joseph John, was born 1857. The record does not mention his place of birth. Anna Losier (Raffensperger) was born in 1859 in Muscatine, Iowa, and Sophie was born in 1860 in Louisville, Kentucky.

Sophie Wedge quotes her mother from the German family Bible. Margarete Anna had written:

> *Gone to everlasting rest, my dear husband [Joseph Losier] and father of 3 helpless small children. Died for his second country. He enlisted as a soldier in Louisville, Kentucky in August 1861. In the battle at Pittsburge Landing [Shiloh] in April 1862 he was shot and badly wounded. He was taken to the hospital in Mount City, Mos. [Missouri] where he died April the 20th, 1862. His shots were in the left side and arm and were the cause of his death at the age of 32 yrs. Sophie Losier followed her father August 26th, 1862. Many tears and many heartaches I indured.*

Kentucky was a slave state and a border state lying between the North and the Deep South. Though there were secessionist groups active in the state, Kentucky stayed in the Union. I believe that Joseph Losier was probably a Union soldier under Grant.

Six months after the death of her husband, Margarete Anna Losier remarried in Indianapolis on October 23, 1863, to Herman William Schowe. Herman was born in Konigrich, Prussia. He and Margarete had five children, their second was "Aunt" Sophie Schowe, born in 1865 and named for Joseph and Margarete's infant daughter Sophie who died in 1862.

The Schowes lived in Indianapolis but were not well received by half-sister Anna as indicated above. They were "poor relations." Sophie Schowe Wedge mentions her mother's pride in her son Joseph John Losier, who was elected a postmaster in Tennessee. Joseph Losier would have been an uncle to Hiram Joseph Raffensperger, and it would seem that Anna named my grandfather after her husband, Hiram, and her father and older brother who were both named Joseph.

Margarete Losier Schowe died in 1911 in Indianapolis. She was seventy-nine. I wonder if my grandfather knew his grandmother. I wonder why her daughter, Anna Losier Raffensperger, was so distant.

Hiram Joseph Raffensperger
(1884–1973)
Lucy Mary Bauer Raffensperger
(1884–1967)

They had a sense of refinement.
They were peaceful, proper, a perfect family . . .
—Alberta's sister

And so we come to Babboo, inheritor of so much fine tradition going back to the earliest days of the city. But it is impossible to write about Lucy Bauer Raffensperger and her husband, Hiram Raffensperger separately. My paternal grandparents were high school sweethearts. Hiram and Lucy—Andad and Babboo to me—were born in Indianapolis and lived there all of their lives. They were married for sixty years.

Hiram and Lucy seem to have enjoyed most pleasant and comfortable childhoods in Indianapolis, having the advantages of parents who were active and prominent in the city. Interacting with other families of German heritage, their parents supported the German organizations and philosophy of education. Both Hiram and Lucy graduated from Manual Training High School in the Class of 1903. Commencement exercises were held that year at English's Opera House on June 8.

Lucy may or may not have been aware that the philosophy of her grandfather's German-English School had influenced the establishment of her high school. Impressed by the success of the innovative programs at the German-English Independent School and at Short-ridge High School, in 1891 the legislature authorized the erection of a manual training school which opened in 1894. Charles E. Emmerich, who had been quite active with the Freethinkers, was made its principal. Manual was the only high school in the country which taught practical training along with the academic subjects. The school's popularity grew until over one thousand students selected this mode of education each year in the early 1900s. Since Emmerich proved to be such an excellent principal, the school was later named for him.

Though my grandmother was musical, her talent apparently didn't rival that of her younger sister Katherine's and she did not study in Europe as Katherine (Tattie) had. She did, however, graduate from the Metropolitan School of Music, where she studied piano. The first Indianapolis music school and an art school were established in 1895 and were originally housed in what had been Henry Ward Beecher's church on the Circle. From these schools evolved the Metropolitan School of Music and the John Herron Art Institute. Lucy must have attended the music school shortly after high school, probably between 1904 and 1906, prior to her marriage.

Hiram was a member of both the varsity basketball and track teams at Manual Training High School. I recall my grandmother showing me news clippings proclaiming his feats on the basketball court, which amazed me when I realized he stood only five feet seven inches tall. When he was in high school, he traveled to New York and was in or around Buffalo at the time of President William McKinley's assassination by an anarchist in 1901. He talked of the event much as we do the assassination of John F. Kennedy today. After graduation from Manual, Hiram worked as a messenger and bookkeeper and then entered advertising work for Ko-We-Ba foods about 1907, the year of his marriage to Lucy Mary Bauer. That same year President Theodore Roosevelt, who succeeded McKinley, came to Indianapolis to dedicate a statue honoring Henry W. Lawton, a Spanish-American War general. Hiram may well have been in the crowd of forty to sixty thousand that gathered to catch a glimpse of their President.

Hiram Raffensperger and Lucy Bauer were married in the home of Lucy's parents, Mr. and Mrs. George Bauer, 2932 N. Illinois Street, at 8 o'clock on April 11, 1907. The Indianapolis newspapers carried detailed descriptions of the event, which Lucy saved in an album she made for her firstborn, Edward. The description reads as follows:

The marriage of Miss Lucy Mary Bauer, daughter of Mr. and Mrs. George Bauer, and Hiram J. Raffensperger took place at the bride's parents, 2932 N. Illinois Street. The guests were the relatives and most intimate friends. The ceremony was performed by the Rev. E. B. Rawls, presiding elder. Before the ceremony, David Levy, now of Danville, pianist, and Kenneth Rose, of Wabash, violinist, played "Dreams," which was changed to the "Lohengrin" wedding march for the entrance of the bridal party, and then to "O, Thou Sublime Sweet Evening Star" for the reading of the service.

The bride and bridegroom entered together and their attendants were Burton Raffensperger, a brother, who was best man; Margaret Clough, a cousin of the bride, was the ring bearer (flower girl). The floral setting for the ceremony was an arch of apple blossoms [the other news article said cherry blossoms] *before a pyramid of palms, and tall cathedral candles.*

The bride wore an exquisite gown of white pineapple gauze made over silk, with a yoke and bertha of needlepoint lace. Her veil was held with orange blossoms, sent by a friend from Arizona, and her bouquet was of white roses. Miss Katherine Bauer, the only sister, was the maid of honor, and she wore a gown of pink silk and carried a cluster of pink roses. The little maid wore a French dress of pink and white and carried pink sweet peas.

The engraved wedding invitation said that they would be "At Home after May first—1420 Fletcher Avenue," but prior to the birth of their first son in 1909, the Raffenspergers moved in with Lucy's parents.

Hiram's brother Arthur followed his father and became a druggist in Indianapolis but, as has been said, Hiram joined his father-in-law's company, Kothe, Wells & Bauer, first in advertising later as a buyer. Hiram rose to serve as vice-president of the wholesale grocery firm and served on its board of directors.

During World War I, Hiram was a young husband with two small sons as well as a member of Company H of the Indiana State Militia. I remember Andad told me a young German woman worked for and lived with the family during the war until they learned that she was a "German spy"! She was quickly dismissed.

After George Bauer's death in 1918, Lucy Bauer Raffensperger inherited her father's interest in Ko-We-Ba, and Hiram stayed with the company. That same year William Kothe's only son, Eugene, died prematurely of the flu while in Washington, D. C. Having expected Eugene to take over the company one day, William Kothe now began to look outside the company for young leadership and hired A. H. Gisler, a graduate of Manual Training High School and Wabash College. Gisler was secretary-treasurer of Grocer's Supply, which Ko-We-Ba absorbed when Kothe hired him as sales manager in 1924. My grandfather had risen to the position of vice-president of Kothe, Wells & Bauer by this time.

William Kothe has been described as "Kaiser Wilhelm himself," apparently a formidable man who ruled the company like a king. He had hired Gisler as sales manager, but Gisler threatened to leave his new position after the following incident: in charge of sales, Gisler had sold "futures" of popular items like canned tomatoes, work gloves, and Ball canning jars. In other words, he had guaranteed shipment of these items to clients at dates in the future. On learning from the shipping department that the futures had not been shipped as promised, Gisler told William Kothe he would prefer to quit if he couldn't have the full cooperation of *all* personnel. Enraged, William Kothe called a meeting of all employees. Going around the room, he pointed to each person, including the top salesman and Hiram Raffensperger, and stated that Al Gisler and *no one else*, was in charge. His orders were to be followed without question.

In 1934 William Kothe named Al Gisler as president, a position Hiram Raffensperger at age fifty might have expected but was denied, perhaps due to his age and the determination of Kothe to promote Gisler, a younger man. At his own suggestion, William Kothe was elected vice-president and chairman of the board of both Kothe, Wells & Bauer Company and Ko-We-Ba Realty Company. An article in *The Indianapolis Star* dated February, 1934 announced Kothe's decision to step aside and listed H. J. Raffensperger as the treasurer of Ko-We-Ba Realty Company, "a holding corporation that owns the real estate occupied by Kothe, Wells & Bauer Company."

The Ko-We-Ba Realty Company had been organized in 1924 when a five-story brick, steel, and concrete building was erected at 240 Virginia Avenue. The building contained seventy-five thousand square feet of floor space and was equipped with all labor-saving devices applicable to the trade. There was a railroad switch on the north side with a capacity of six cars. On the south side twenty-five hundred feet was set aside for use in loading motor vehicles. Ko-We-Ba also owned buildings in Wabash and Kokomo, Indiana, where branches of the firm had been established.

By 1934 the trademark name, Ko-We-Ba, under which Kothe, Wells & Bauer sold their products, was a household word for quality merchandise throughout the Midwest. George Bauer would have been proud of the progress made and the success of his company. The company was selling its own full line of canned goods, coffee roasted in its plant, spices, tea, extracts and other high grade food products. And thus the business continued through the early forties.

Following World War II the stockholders of Ko-We-Ba Realty requested a rent increase from the parent company. As the building was now dated and inadequate for the needs of a more modern wholesale grocery business, the request was denied and Ko-We-Ba Company called in all its preferred stock in 1947. Stockholders received $103 per share. The Realty Company was dissolved and its buildings were subsequently sold. In 1950 Ko-We-Ba built a new warehouse. Four years later, Al Gisler's son and namesake took over as president and gradually bought out the remaining interests of the Kothe family, who, unlike the Raffenspergers, maintained common stock in the company. In 1978 Ko-We-Ba was sold to Continental Foods which was subsequently sold to Sysco Corporation, a Texas company, around 1990.

Al Gisler, Jr., remembered that Ko-We-Ba products carried the logo "Ko-We-Ba Means the Best." A rumor started at some point that "Ko-We-Ba" was an Indian name. During his tenure as president he received several phone calls from people saying they had been named "Ko-We-Ba" because it meant "the best" and wanting to know more about the derivation of the Indian name translated as "superior, or the best." It got a little complicated to explain.

Not only was Hiram Raffensperger affiliated with Kothe, Wells & Bauer Company, but he was also a participant in the formation of Merz Engineering Company in 1927, along with several other local businessmen including Reilly Adams, president of the Security Trust Company, and Fred Moskovics, president of Stutz Motor Company. The purpose of the company was to study and later manufacture aviation motors for commercial use. The plant was located at 200 S. Harding Street and was headed by Charles C. Merz, a former race car driver. Hiram served as financial advisor. It was because of his connection with Merz that he and his college-aged sons spent a lot of time at the Indianapolis Motor Speedway in the thirties, frequently serving as scorekeepers during time trials and on Race day.

By 1938 Merz had developed a steam-powered rotary motor suitable for cars or planes. Independent testing was to be conducted at Purdue University and Merz began production within the year. In 1950 the physical assets of the Merz Company were sold to Love Machine Corporation. At the time Merz had over a hundred employees, and the new owner continued to operate both plants. Hiram was affiliated with Merz until 1955. By 1969 Merz was manufacturing heavy machine products, dies, special machinery such as missile parts, and testing and gauging equipment.

I had always been under the impression my grandfather retired at forty-five, after having been told by a fortune teller that he wouldn't live a long life! Though he may not have worked full time, he did not retire and he definitely had a long life. Perhaps one reason for his longevity was another one of his wife Lucy's many talents—her cooking. I loved eating at their home. My grandmother, Babboo, prepared delicious meals, many of which I still recreate. I adored her tomato juice, made from both red and yellow homegrown tomatoes, and her stewed tomatoes with bread. A favorite family dinner was the German dish sauerbraten accompanied by noodles with buttered bread crumbs. Often, dessert was Black John Pudding, a very dark European sweet steamed pudding made with molasses. My favorite breakfast was Babboo's "milk toast," lightly toasted white bread served with warm milk and sugar.

Christmastime meant Babboo's springerle cookies. These were

German anise cakes, each stamped with a picture using a wooden mold. For our family Christmas dinner, she always made red cabbage to accompany the turkey, and plum pudding with its two scrumptious sauces, hard sauce and "soupy" sauce, both made of butter, sugar, and eggs.

Everyone in the family, especially Ed and I, craved her incredibly sweet "Kiss Pie" at any time of the year, yet I have never been able to duplicate what seems a simple recipe:

Kiss Pie

- Prepare and prebake a 9-inch pie crust.
- Fill half of the crust with granulated sugar and a rounded tablespoon of flour.
- Add a *tiny* pinch of salt.
- Pour milk over the sugar mixture 1/2 inch from top of crust.
- Stir with fingers so as not to break the crust. Dot with one tablespoon of butter. Sprinkle with nutmeg.

  Place in 400 degree oven for 10 minutes. Reduce temperature to 350 and bake until the custard thickens. Don't overcook. Cool on a wire rack.

It has been suggested that Babboo forgot the eggs when she gave me the recipe, but I have yet to try the recipe with that addition.

With her sewing skills, Lucy made many of her own clothes and from the scraps made doll clothes for me. She also crocheted; we still enjoy one of her marvelous multicolored wool afghans. In addition to being a wonderful homemaker and mother, Lucy was active in the community. I believe she particularly enjoyed her long affiliation with the Saturday Afternoon Literary Club.

Lucy Raffensperger was extremely well-organized, a good club woman, and like her husband she appreciated nature and travel. Hiram was an excellent photographer. Family activities and vacations are recorded in black and white prints, 16 mm. movies and color slides. These two kept wonderful photograph albums, which I treasure.

As a wholesale grocer, Hiram was curious about new products and loved to grocery shop. He and Babboo kept a well-stocked freezer of meats and fresh-frozen vegetables carefully wrapped in white freezer paper dated and labelled with red or black marking crayons. Hiram also enjoyed making hors d'oeuvres for parties and knew how to wield a pastry tube. A wonderful gardener, he prepared a vegetable garden as well as flower beds each spring. There were always zinnias for cutting and the yard smelled of tube roses and lilies of the valley. Andad grew spectacular tomatoes of several varieties, and Babboo canned what couldn't be eaten. His green thumb was passed down to his youngest son.

Hiram liked to drive; the family had one of the first electric cars in Indianapolis. The cars I remember best were their Cadillacs, always dark blue. Though they were a two-car family (Babboo had a Ford), Andad was the driver. I think Babboo could drive, but she never did so when I was in the car. When I started teaching school in the fall of 1961, my grandfather and grandmother gave me Babboo's latest car, a '58 Ford two-tone light green sedan.

In 1943 World War II was at its peak. My father, Bill Raffensperger, was in the Navy in the South Pacific. Andad worked with the Marion County Ration Board, becoming its director. And I was three. My grandmother very much wanted to keep the memory of my father alive for me and attempted to by relating to me time and again stories which formed a chronicle of my father's childhood. It wasn't until after her death that I discovered a written version, a portion of which I include here:

The Story About Daddy

Once there was a little boy whose name was Edward. He lived with his Daddy and his mother. They were a happy family. One day he asked his mother if she wouldn't please find a baby for him as he would like to have a playmate. She said she would ask the doctor to see if he knew of a nice baby. Well, the doctor called and said he could bring the baby in June. Edward was so sure that he was going to have a little sister that he decided to name the baby Suzanne. Mother told him that he had better find a boy's name too, but he said he was going to call it Suzanne anyway.

One morning Edward was playing and heard a little baby crying. Sure enough, he had a little new brother and his name was George William Raffensperger. Edward was a funny boy and said he was going to call the baby Suzanne anyway. Mother and Daddy called the baby Billy but when he began to try to talk, he could not say "Billy" but said "Budie" so they called him "Budie" but do you know Edward still called him Suzanne!

One day they saw a little boy with yellow hair across the street who seemed to be a nice little boy, so they asked him to come over and play and to bring his sister. Their names were David and Betty Burns, and they all grew to be the best of chums and had the best times together.

Edward, Betty, and David went to school before Billy was old enough, so he found friends in nature to play with. He had the cutest little guinea pig named Jackie that he loved so much and the little thing loved him and would follow him all over the house and if his cage was put out of the sun room, he would cry until he was brought back with the family. Sometimes after a rainstorm, little baby birds would be washed out of their nests and do you know what Budie would do? He would gather them up and bring them into his room and feed them until they were old enough to take care of themselves. Sometimes when Budie was out in the yard, a little bird would fly to him and perch on his shoulder. I think they knew how he loved them and were not afraid. Sometimes he brought tadpole eggs in from a little stream & they would hatch out in a bowl of water in his room. After awhile, they would turn into little frogs & live out in the pool in the garden.

. . . Finally Billy was getting to be a big boy. He and David decided they wanted to buy a car but they were not old enough to drive one yet, so they finally said if they could make some money and buy a car that they would just put it in the backyard and just pretend they were driving. Do you know what they did to make some money? They built a stand of boxes on the sidewalk and sold cokes to men working on the streets. After awhile they saved enough money to buy a used Ford and Daddy went down and brought it up for them and put it in the backyard. There the two boys would sit, and sometimes they would let Ed-

ward sit in it with them They were so proud of their Ford and I think they were pretty smart little boys to buy a car all by themselves . . .

Hearing these stories of my father's "idyllic" childhood always made me feel that he had been most fortunate. There must have been bad times, but I never heard about them. Many times I thought I would have liked growing up as my father had—I knew his parents were wonderful! Finding and reading this child's family history so many years later, I realize my paternal grandmother was also telling me about herself and her life as a wife and young mother.

In the story Babboo mentions singing the lullaby "Let's Go A-Hunting" to her little boys. The sweet, multi-versed song about Robbin's and Bobbin's hunt had been passed from mother to mother in her family. I sang "Let's Go A-Hunting" to my children, who loved it and asked me to sing it over and over. Considering my inability to carry a tune, I was flattered. I won't be surprised to hear my children singing about Robbin and Bobbin to their babies.

The house Babboo referred to in her stories about Billy is a large three-story house at 4240 Washington Boulevard. Even today it is in a wonderful neighborhood of lovely old historic houses and 4240 is only a couple of blocks north of the childhood home of my husband, Dave Fauvre, at 4050 Washington Boulevard.

My father's friend Dave Burns became an architect like his father, Lee, and in 1956 designed a one-story French Provincial style house for Bill and his wife at 6020 Sunset Lane in Indianapolis. It was, at the time, my parents "dream house." He and Bill had a wonderful annual tradition, which I believe started after the war, of having lunch together every Christmas Eve.

Over the years, although Dave Burns and his wife Jessie socialized more with my uncle Ed and his wife Alberta, I always thought of Dave as my father's best friend. Immediately following my father's funeral in 1976, the first person I recognized through my tears was Jessie. Though we were not that close and had not seen each other for years, to me she represented David Burns, who was one of the pall bearers and out of sight at that sad moment. I found myself sobbing in her arms and remembering the little yellow-haired boy who played with my father, whom my grandmother had immortalized in her stories.

But as all little boys do, Hiram and Lucy's grew up. Babboo wanted to also share their growing-up time with me in her story:

> One day he came home and said, "Mur, I met a girl today and she was the sweetest girl I ever saw." They went to dances together and to shows and parties and the girl thought that Billy was the nicest boy she had ever seen. Who do you suppose that girl was? She was Eunice Mae Howell.
>
> One day he came to them and said, "Folks, you know I love Eunice Mae and we want to be married." Mur and Daddy knew she was a nice girl and told them if they were sure they loved each other, that it was all right. Then they asked the girl's mother and daddy and they said it was all right, so they had the prettiest wedding in a big church and went to housekeeping by themselves and were so happy.

Of course, that's not quite the way Bill and Eunice Mae told the story, but Babboo's version was good enough for a three year old! Now returning to Babboo's story:

> One day Eunice Mae said, "Folks, we have something to tell you; we have ordered a baby." And Edward said, "If it is a little girl baby, I am going to call her 'Karen.' " The family waited and waited. The day after Christmas [1939], Eunice Mae went to the hospital and there was the sweetest little baby you ever saw and her name was Beverly Howell Raffensperger. Edward still said he was going to call her 'Karen,' and he did!

My grandparents' home, a three-story house in Crows Nest, holds wonderful memories for me. Built on a hillside above White River, the large house was whitewashed brick with dark green shutters, a screened porch, and a walkout basement. In the summer canvas awnings were put on the windows. Their yard was a child's delight, an acre or two of rolling lawn and large trees and a long driveway running along the north property line. The property and neighborhood off Spring Mill Road adjacent to Holliday Park had been "Camp Felicity" in the late 1880s. Lucy saved this undated clipping from *The Indianapolis News*:

> Booth Tarkington's early ambition to become an artist is brought to mind in glancing through an old guest book belonging to Miss Elizabeth Claypool, which lists the many camping parties and club picnics which were entertained at the Claypool "Camp Felicity" out at Crow's Nest . . . The eminent author's signature, which appears in several parties, is accompanied by hilarious sketches, such as a Maypole group with highly dramatized names on May 1, 1887; a skull and crossbones decorates one of his signatures, and a clever profile of the author himself, which isn't a bad likeness today.
>
> Judge Solomon Claypool started the camp in '86, to fill the need for a picnic and camping ground for visiting groups, and names of our old first families appear frequently in the pages of the guest book . . . Then there is the annual picnic of the advanced department of the Girls' Classical School, May 21, 1887; a picnic of the Fortnightly Literary Club June 22, 1886, and other interesting mementos of a former day.

The name Claypool was well known in Indianapolis, principally connected with the old Claypool Hotel downtown. The family built a house on the Camp Felicity property around 1878 and entertained family and friends there, cutting a road to the house for their horse and buggy. Water was brought up from the spring in buckets and pulled up the hill with pulleys. When the Claypool children grew up, married, and moved away, the Claypools moved closer to downtown Indianapolis. The house was left deserted, vandalized, and taken over by vagrants, or as Lucy put it, "tramps."

Hiram and Lucy rediscovered the Claypool property while driving in their car "up a narrow deserted road" in the early 1930s. They fell in love with the area and after the property was sectioned into one to three acre homesites they built their own house on the side of the hill. The small community was named North Crow's Nest.

Hiram and Lucy were in their mid-fifties when they decided to sell their large three-story home on Washington Boulevard and build at

6161 Sunset Lane. Their sons were married, they were soon to have a grandchild, and World War II loomed on the horizon.

The original Claypool house was torn down. It had been located where the Raffenspergers planted their flower and vegetable garden near the end of the driveway. Hiram and Lucy decided to leave a little cedar tree, which had stood at the corner of the porch of the Claypool house, "just as a marker for the old home," my grandmother wrote. An old post, "all that was left of the fence that once protected the [Claypool] house and yard around it," was also saved by the Raffenspergers.

Babboo and Andad loved entertaining, and their beautiful home was always open to their sons, their wives and friends. Ed and Bill entertained their friends at their parents with "steak fries and wienie roasts." Lucy wrote that "each year we had a group of our young friends for dinner during the winter, and each summer we had a Sunday breakfast and they usually stayed all day."

Though it's been forty-five years since I was last in 6161 Sunset Lane, I could draw a fairly accurate floor plan. I loved that big house, but more importantly I loved the people who lived there, so my memories are attached to warm feelings. Hiram and Lucy Raffensperger's house, with its rolling lawn, huge trees, and gardens still looks grand to me, though not as large as I once thought. The house is no longer white, the brick has become its natural color, but the woods are still there, as is White River below.

Holliday Park, adjacent to the residential area commonly referred to as Crow's Nest, bounded the property just north of my grandparents'. I loved to walk in those spacious, tree-dotted grounds with Babboo and Andad Raffensperger to picnic and feed the goldfish which lived in a large pond in the park. To reach the park all we had to do was walk to the end of the street and squeeze through some high bushes. When I grew older and went to the park with my boyfriend, I was surprised to discover that Holliday Park was more than an immense green with trees and a fish pond. The park also included a woods with interesting walking trails leading down to the river. The Raffenspergers' house on the hill would still be considered in a prime location south of Meridian Hills Country Club and Holliday Park.

Babboo and I never tired of talking about what the property was like in the days of the Indians who camped and hunted along the River before white settlers moved them to the West. I loved to hear stories of how my grandparents found arrowheads during the excavation of their house. Touching the arrowheads themselves stimulated my imagination.

Babboo encouraged my curiosity about Indian lore and nature on her wooded hill, and I loved to pretend that I too would find evidence of Indians on Sunset Lane. In 1948 Babboo wrote a book about life in Crow's Nest and my part in sharing it with them. She called it *Beverly Hill at Crow's Nest,* and in it she recounted all of my favorite stories of Indians and the woods animals. I was eight when she presented me with the book and I still treasure it some forty-six years later. Babboo made copies by hand in 1948 and gave them to my two close child-hood friends, Elizabeth Steele and Jane Gant. Liz and Jane loved my grandparents and their beautiful home nearly as much as I. We all looked forward to going "around the corner, over the bridge, and up the hill to Babboo and Andad's house." (Liz and I lived on Fifty-ninth Street between Illinois and Meridian. Jane lived just north of Fifty-sixth and Illinois.)

We girls didn't refer to 6161 Sunset Lane as "Beverly Hill"—it was always just Babboo and Andad's. And what fun we had. In the summer we were pioneers or Indians and in the fall "architects" designing terrific floor plans of leaves.

Babboo wrote of these adventures, and when I reread her book, I can again smell the newly-mown grass, the damp earth and the burning leaves. I can see the vegetable garden and the summer flowers, colorful zinnias being my favorites, and I remember walks in the woods, the wildflowers, the "Jesus Tree" where they hung a crucifix, and the river, where Indians once camped. One of Babboo's chapters gives the flavor of both the place and personality of this remarkable Bauer woman:

Pioneers or Indians

The river gets very high in the Spring and flows past our woods with an angry roar. It does not look as if it should be called White River but when the Indians named it that, it was clear and clean. It flowed over a white rock bed and really looked white; but after all these years when the soil was washing down into it and it overflowed its banks, the white rock bed was covered with mud, so that is seldom even clean any more. Our house stands over a hundred feet above the river so we are never in danger of having it come close to us, but it surely goes on the rampage sometimes and does a lot of damage where the ground is low. Even though the water is muddy, it looks like molten silver when it flows down in the sun. Sometimes very early in the morning when it is a shimmering sheet of silver, I am almost sure that I can see that canoe again, gliding quietly down the stream, and of course, I am just as sure that it is Hiawatha. It may be just a branch of a tree washing down stream, but it could be a canoe. Most folks would not see it because they do not dream like you and I do.

Our little girls love to play in a make-believe world. Sometimes they are Indians, sometimes, pioneers. It is fun to pull your imaginary canoe up on the bank, climb up to the top of the hill, and to find much to your surprise, a flat hill top that is a perfect place to build your tee-pee. Pictures are drawn on big sheets of brown paper, three long sticks are tied together at the top, and set up. The paper is put over them and a sheet is draped above that. Lots of folks would think it is a sheet but it is really wild animal skins. Next a fire has to be built and of course a real fire would not be safe, so colored paper is a very real substitute and everything is ready for the wild duck, wild turkey, and deer that the hunters have gone out after.

Sometimes they prefer to be pioneers and the play is much the same except that the pioneers have to be on the alert constantly because of Indians. Your canoe has been wrecked in the angry waters and you had to swim ashore, losing almost all your belongings. A tee-pee or a sort of lean-to is built and about the same things happen, because the [white] men who came to these wilds first had to live just like the Indians did and were always in fear of them [or so believed three little imaginative girls].

I do not know where the pioneers [Elizabeth and Beverly] *found the cow which I noticed being milked but one was produced somehow, and the very modern name of Ballerino was given it. Lunches served on Navy trays, of peanut butter and bacon sandwiches, sliced tomatoes, fresh apple sauce, carrot strips, seedless grapes, bananas, and milk, are not exactly pioneer rations, but they taste pretty good anyway. The bugs are the greatest menace these poor men encounter, so life in the wild woods is not too rugged after all.*

Nothing captures Babboo's personality, love of nature, children, and animals as her stories in *Beverly Hill at Crows Nest*. Another chapter in Babboo's book explains the Jesus Tree:

The Jesus Tree

Many years ago when we took our boys and traveled around Europe, we found that every forest in France had its Virgin Tree. It usually stood apart from the others or towered above them, and there was always a large wreath or a cross with the crucified Christ on the side of the tree. It seemed to us a beautiful way to honor the Mother of Jesus and when we bought our hill, we decided to honor Her in the same way. We selected a huge buckeye tree which stood alone on the lookout point, overlooking the woods and the river, but still was a secluded spot where we could go and be alone with God and pray. The ground was covered with myrtle and all was quiet except for the murmur of the river way below and a light rustle of leaves overhead; and there we hung our cross with the figure of Christ.

Years later when we were deep in World War II and our boys were in the service in the Navy, that spot was a haven to us and to our little Beverly, who was only about three years old at that time. She grieved for her Daddy and for her Uncle Ed and worried constantly for fear her Daddy would never come home from the South Pacific.

It was here I found her one day when she had disappeared while I was picking flowers along the path the tree; here under the cross she was kneeling and praying in her baby lisp, that her Daddy would come back safe. She went there many times all of her own accord and seemed to find a certain comfort from going. She named it her "Jesus Tree" and so it will always be.

My grandparents and their sons loved animals, particularly dogs. When their sons were little, they had a fox terrier. In 1928 Ed's fiancé Alberta gave him a German Shepherd named Dawn who stole the family's heart and was featured in an article about aristocratic dogs which appeared in *The Indianapolis News* in 1931:

> *Many pedigreed dogs are owned by Indianapolis women. They date their ancestry back to some of the most aristocratic in the canine world. Dawn, for instance, the beautiful German police dog belonging to H. Edward Raffensperger, is a nephew of Strongheart, of movie fame, and could probably flash across the silver screen as creditably as his celebrated uncle, if fate had thrown such training his way. He can at least boast of a marvelously strong family resemblance. As his master is away at college, the care of Dawn falls to Mrs. Hiram J. Raffensperger, and loyally does he repay her kindness. Known as a one-family dog, Dawn is especially devoted to his mistress, and is one of those who "can do anything but talk."*

Dawn didn't live to join the Raffenspergers at Crows Nest. His death was so painful to them that neither they nor Ed ever owned another dog. They did, however, accept everyone else's dogs, and there were always puppy bones available for neighborhood visitors. They nursed injured dogs, squirrels and birds and had many animal friends who loved these kind and gentle people.

Summers were especially meaningful for the Raffenspergers. When their sons were young they spent time at Lake Wawasee in northern Indiana and camped in Wisconsin. At Wawasee they visited with the Lilly family and became friends with Charlie Brien, the unofficial "admiral" of the lake. Perhaps it was at Wawasee that Ed and Bill learned to love the water, which influenced their decisions to join the Navy during World War II.

I loved summers at my grandparents on Sunset Lane. Actually, I loved any time of year on their hill. There were bird and squirrel feeders, a huge old fire bell which hung from a wooden frame, and, of course, a swing for their granddaughter. The dining room had a heavy oak dining table with matching chairs and buffet, which I inherited in 1968. It continues to this day to be the scene of many parties and family dinners. If only it could talk of its fifty years in the Raffensperger family! The screened-in porch on the back of the house was a favorite place, cool and comfortable during the summer months, with metal porch furniture all green and white. I especially loved the glider.

The stairway to the third floor, or second story, curved to the left. There were three bedrooms of varying sizes, the largest being my grandparents'. The guest bedrooms were separated from the master bedroom by an open library. The only piece of furniture remaining today from the library is an antique rocker that originated with the Bauers. The highly carved oak rocker with a curved spindled back remains in the family.

I always slept in the large guest room, with its beautiful dark walnut four poster bed. Before I went to sleep Babboo climbed into bed next to me and read or told me stories. One of my favorites was the popular *Uncle Wiggly* series, and I always loved *Jiggers*, the children's book about a lost dog. But I also listened intently to her stories of family or early Indiana history. I was fascinated with the story of Frances Slocum, a little white Quaker girl who was kidnapped by the Delaware Indians near Wilkes-Barre, Pennsylvania, in 1778 and raised by them in Ohio and Michigan. Frances later married a Miami chief and continued living the life of an Indian in a settlement near Peru, Indiana. It was there that she was discovered some sixty years after her capture. Though reunited with family members in 1837, she chose to remain as she had lived, an Indian. However, when the rest of her tribe was forced to move West, Congress granted Frances one square mile around her home and improvements "in fee to her and her heirs forever."

Babboo told me the story of Frances Slocum as often as I asked and included the story in her book, *Beverly Hill at Crows Nest*. It was a story I would never forget, though her rendition included only the highlights, just enough to tantalize a child. In 1992, I met a Cleo Slocum from San Jose, California, and quickly inquired if she was related to the famous Frances Slocum of Peru, Indiana. She told me that her husband Donald was a descendent of one of Frances' white brothers. Don and Cleo had visited Peru and the Slocum monument and when there had actually met the great-granddaughter of Frances Slocum, a Mrs. Bundy. Cleo said that she could see a family resemblance. Mrs. Slocum sent me a copy of a wonderful narrative of the Frances Slocum story written by Edward S. Ellis entitled *The Lost Sister of Wyoming*. I read the detailed account with as much enthusiasm as I had listened to and read my grandmother's story some fifty years ago.

After reading Edward Ellis's history, I commented to Cleo that I found one discrepancy in the two tales. Lucy Raffensperger translated Ma-Con-A-Qua, Frances's Indian name, as White Rose. Mr. Ellis said it meant "Young Bear." Cleo responded, "I like the translation of 'white rose' rather than 'young bear,' although if she (Frances) was like the rest of the Slocums she was probably more like a bear." Ma-Con-A-Qua means little bear in the Miami language.

As you can tell my grandmother had a tremendous influence on me as a child and probably is responsible for instilling in me an interest in American history, as well as an appreciation for the woods, flowers, and wildlife. I also enjoyed the companionship of my grandfather, Hiram. I can still picture Andad sitting in his dark blue chair in a sunny spot listening to a football game with me sitting or playing at his feet. I also remember trying to curl Andad's straight, short, and thinning grey hair by attempting to create waves with hair clips. He was a most patient grandfather as I played hair dresser and giggled with Babboo.

About the only negative thing I can recall of my days spent at 6161 Sunset Lane was a recurring nightmare of a wolf which chased me out of the woods and into the dark, two-car garage. I'd dream this, scream for my grandparents and then awaken. While there were foxes sighted occasionally in the woods, I never saw one, and there were no wolves. My grandparents and their homes were always a safe haven for me, even when I grew older.

On April 21, 1950, Babboo wrote a postscript to *Beverly Hill at Crow's Nest*:

This morning we stood at our bedroom window, overlooking the river and the woods we love so well, and realized that a change has come into our lives that will take us away from Beverly Hill; and yet for some reason we are not grieving. We are older now [sixty-six] and our duties here, living in a three-story house on the side of a hill, have become too strenuous . . .

We decided, after a great deal of thought, that we need a house all on one floor with a small yard that Andad can garden without wearing himself out. We are leaving the hill in just a little while now to stay in an apartment at 3540 N. Meridian St., sort of playing housekeeping while we are building and are as happy as two children. We will not be far from our river and have been invited back to our woods whenever we care to come. We had a surprise yesterday when Andad found another arrowhead right in our new yard, so you see we are not going very far from our old camping ground and the Indians lived there too. We will not have our trees but we are close to Holliday Park and we can run over here often; but since we cannot climb hills much longer, we may just live in memories of our hill. We have had sickness and health, and heart-aches and happiness in this house, and have lived each moment to the fullest, with never a regret that we came here and never a regret that we are leaving.

Beverly [age ten] grieves but she will love the new house I am sure, for it will be filled with the same furniture, the same love and contentment that fills this one. She turned the first spade of earth at 6845 N. Delaware St. as we all gathered there on Easter morning [the whole family, including my maternal grandparents, the Howells] *to begin another era in our lives and surely there could be no better day to do it.*

We are glad that the redbuds are not out, and that the birds have not returned; it is not nearly so hard to part with the woods as if Spring had brought all her flowers and birds and animals to lay at our feet. Our neighbors to the south have promised to feed our little friends and not to allow any harm to come to them if they can avoid it, so we are leaving, looking forward to happiness and better health in our new little stone house with Andad's flower and vegetable garden, where the birds will come to get their food, and where our friends, both young and old, will always be so welcome, and where our children will find "home" just as it has always been.

I do remember the ground-breaking for Babboo and Andad's new house in Arden, not far from Ed and Alberta's home on Warwick Road, where I did again experience the "love and contentment" I had found in Crows Nest. But I always missed the woods and the grandeur of 6161 Sunset Lane. It was to this new house that I again brought my friends, including my boyfriend, Dave Fauvre, in 1954. We had wonderful times with my grandparents, and he quickly grew to love them too. The new house had a shuffleboard court in the basement and that was always great fun.

Though architecturally a simple fifties-style limestone, it was not a small house. It had a good-sized living room and dining room, two large bedrooms and a full basement. Andad again had flowers and a vegetable garden. He made his own compost as he always had. There was a bird feeder, but no swing. The screened porch was eventually enclosed, creating a den/library where we usually gathered after dinner to get out the old family photo albums or watch television.

Andad, whose eyesight began to fail, still enjoyed listening to the radio. He always had a large radio next to his bed which had short-wave capability. In his bedroom closet was a rifle, carefully hung out of reach on a gun rack. Babboo kept her old treadle sewing machine in one of the large guestroom closets. In the other, she kept her clothes.

The year I was born, 1939, was a watershed for the German American community of my heritage. Indianapolis' German American families, though not as closely tied to their heritage as their parents and grandparents had been in 1915, were once again faced with fighting a war with their fatherland. During World War II, Hiram and Lucy were a source of strength and comfort to their sons and their families. Lucy wrote in the last pages of *The Story About Daddy*.

After awhile there was a bad war and Daddy decided he would have to go to fight the bad Nazis and Japs. He went away to school at Cornell and one day Beverly and Momey and Andad and Babboo got in their car and went to Ithaca to see him. Then he came home to Andad and Babboo's house for he had rented their new house to people till the war was over. Then one day Daddy, Momey, and Beverly all packed up and went to Norfolk. Babboo cried when her two chums went away on the train. They could not find a place to live in Norfolk so Momey and Beverly went to Richmond, Virginia, to live and Daddy could come over there and see them. Then Beverly and Momey came home and after awhile Momey went to see Daddy again and Beverly stayed with Babboo and Andad till time to go to Tallahassee (Florida), where Momey had found a little house. Babboo and Andad took her on the train. Finally they arrived in Tallahassee and Momey and Daddy were waiting for the train to hug their precious baby girl to them. They were so happy to be together and Babboo and Andad were glad to spend Christmas there too . . .

Hiram and Lucy treated me as they had their sons—with complete devotion. They were interesting, warm people, but it was not just to their family that they gave of their time and energy. They also gave to their friends and community. When I was in my teens, Andad served Indianapolis' Mayor Clark as president of the Indianapolis Board of Park Commissioners. He was responsible for bringing the steam engine to Broad Ripple Park, and it was during his term as president that the Hilton U. Brown outdoor theatre was built. The theatre, named for the former editor of *The Indianapolis News*, became the home of the "Starlight Musicals," a popular summer series in Indianapolis. The Olympic Swimming Trials were held at Broad Ripple Park one summer, and one of the Hawaiian swim coaches so enjoyed Hiram that he invited the Raffenspergers to Hawaii. Though approaching their seventies, they made the long trip and were entertained by the Hawaiians in true "aloha" fashion.

I recall that when Andad and Babboo phoned from Oahu, they sounded a half a world away, but it was exciting to hear from them and be in touch. Hiram and Lucy loved to travel and never forgot to bring back something for their only grandchild. I enjoyed maple sugar candy from their trips to New England and the real cotton pod they brought me from somewhere in the South.

The Raffenspergers loved Christmas and taught my mother how festive the holiday could be. They were generous and creative with their gifts, as photographs testify, and it was the Raffenspergers who started the Christmas traditions our family treasure to this day. Until I was born in 1939, and again during the war years, Christmases were always celebrated at the Raffenspergers'. My stronger memories, however, are of all the wonderful Christmases at my childhood home on Fifty-ninth Street, with my grandparents present.

They would arrive on Christmas Eve with a laundry basket of wrapped gifts to put under our tree. After they left and stockings were hung, my father would hang a sheet across the entry to our living room in anticipation of Santa's arrival. Early Christmas morning, my grandparents returned to our house on Fifty-ninth Street to watch me discover what Santa brought and to exchange gifts. After the gift exchange, they would return home to change into more formal clothes, returning Christmas afternoon for the traditional turkey dinner, which featured Babboo's homemade red cabbage and plum pudding.

Semiretired and comfortable financially, the Raffenspergers were mainstays of their family. Their relationship with both sons was close and they seemed to me to be the one real constant in my life; they were never far away in any sense. Lucy wrote when they traveled and when we traveled. When I vacationed with my parents, there were always letters from Babboo awaiting us when we arrived at our destination. She wrote much as she talked, inspirational and encouraging to all.

When I graduated from high school in 1957, my Raffensperger grandparents presented me with a small diamond ring. Set in a contemporary gold and silver mounting, the diamond had been my Great-Aunt Tattie's engagement diamond. I received several pieces of beautiful jewelry from my grandmother, but this ring, I knew, was memorable. Babboo's letter that accompanied this gift was autobiographical and typical of her.

June 7, 1957

Dear Precious:

We know what an eventful night this is in the life of our dear little granddaughter, for just 54 years ago tomorrow, Andad & I graduated from Emmerich Manual Training High School. Our class motto was

"We finish but to begin" and as the years go by, we realize how true those words are. We finish babyhood, only to begin girl-hood, there on to woman-hood, parent-hood and so on to Eternity. Life is a cycle, each step climbing to a higher level and to higher aspirations. We must always have a goal; we must always be reaching for the stars, so to speak, for when interest in higher ideals lag interest in life fades too.

I am reminded of a little poem that a teacher of mine in the fourth grade asked the class to commit to memory and to repeat it always when we were discouraged.

Over and over again: No matter which way I turn,
I always find in the Book of Life, some lesson that I must learn.
I must take my turn at the mill, I must grind out the golden grain:
I must be at my task with a hearty good will, over and over again.

You will find that all through life, there is a challenge. It is the man who shirks responsibility who is the failure, not the man who keeps trying, even without success. With love, loyalty, true sincerity (and there is a difference) and integrity, which have always been outstanding qualities in your character, you will never go far wrong.

You have had problems already in your young life— we all have had—but with God's help, see to it that the grain is golden that you grind.

You have worked hard for the honors you have received and we are grateful for the joy you have given us from the minute you came into our lives. We are giving you this ring as a token of our love and pride in you. The center diamond was Tattie's from Clarke, and I know how happy they would be to know that you have it. It is a symbol of love: please cherish it and us, in your corner of happy memories.

On the occasion of my marriage Babboo wrote:

June 15, 1960

Dear Precious:
This will be the last time I will be able to give my little girl "spending money" to take on a trip as I have always done, so here it is. When you

leave this time, it will be as a grown-up married woman, and I am sure, a happy one. I know you do not need this, but just for old times' sake, please use it.

Your happiness means almost more than life itself to Andad and me, for you have always been a perfect joy to us. We love David too and are looking forward to a full and happy life for both of you. Now we have two grandchildren and we love it.

I wrote a note to Elizabeth [Elizabeth Steele Creveling, my closest friend who had married the year before] *and she and Bea* [Elizabeth's mother] *want me to repeat it to you. It is the formula for a good life together that has been handed down in our family for ages and is most worthwhile.*

Always talk things over calmly, no matter what the difficulty may be, and never go to sleep at night until you have reached an understanding of love and forgiveness. No two people live life through without some stormy weather, but never let it become a habit. Constant bickering has wrecked many marriages, but this is not like either of you. Tell each other of your love by acts as well as words, for acts of gentleness and appreciation and unselfishness are the things that really count. Never, never let jealousy creep into your hearts.

Remember that David's mother loves him, but in a different way from the feeling you have for him; and remember, above all, that David's love for his mother is entirely different from the love he bears for you, his wife. They cannot be compared in any way, so meet David's mother in that way, knowing that mothers-in-law want the love of the girls their sons marry more than you realize until perhaps you have a son of your own. It will make all of you happy and I am sure David will remember the same tokens toward your parents. There can be so much happiness that Love makes all the difference in the world. Respect each other's wishes and feelings and always preserve a tender dignity toward each other.

Life is seldom smooth through the years, but as long as you have each other, you can solve any problem with God's help. Love and unselfishness are the real key notes to happiness, health and success, so always try to keep that in mind. We are proud of both you and David and you know the faith we have in you. Always remember that every good and perfect gift comes from God and never forget to be grateful to Him for your blessings and thank Him. This morning at Communion, Father Daniel prayed for God's blessing on you and David and Andad and I add our prayers for a good, worthwhile life, of love, health and success for both of you—and now God bless and keep you both always.

Love, Babboo

When I was married at age twenty, Babboo and Andad were seventy-six years old. It was wonderful to have my grandparents at our wedding, and we both so appreciated their blessing. I realize now that Babboo really did think of me as her little girl. Having had two sons, I suspect she would have liked to have had a little girl too and I became that third child. I have always felt that I was raised by four parents.

As to Babboo's advice for newlyweds, she was certainly an idealist! But she must have followed her own advice, for she and Andad were happily married for sixty years. As to whether or not my friend Elizabeth and I followed her advice, I can't speak for Liz, but I know I have gone to bed angry many times. But Liz and I received the blessings given. We have both experienced difficult times in our marriages, but they have been good, solid marriages. We are both still happily married—to our first husbands—after thirty-five years.

Babboo and Andad never bickered much in my presence, and their marriage has always been an inspiration to me and my husband. They always seemed to be happy and fulfilled, individually and together. They both appreciated the same things and seemed nearly inseparable. The only differences I remember was Andad's tendency to want to "go" when Babboo wanted to "stay."

Babboo could be domineering at times, but her family loved her in their different ways. I know my mother sometimes resented Babboo's influence and what she considered her interference, but I know she also admired her.

I believe that Babboo attended the Presbyterian Church as a young adult, and I know that at one time in her life she studied Christian Science, but when St. Paul's Episcopal Church was built at Sixtieth and North Meridian Streets, the entire Raffensperger family joined.

The Raffenspergers were all very active at St. Paul's during the 1950s and 1960s, serving the church in many ways. I don't think of my grandparents as religious people, but they both had a deep faith in God. I found them open-minded and tolerant of different points of view. Babboo's faith helped her get through the stormy periods in her life, the tragic loss of her younger sister, the fear of losing her sons during World War II, my father's bouts with alcoholism and her own poor health later in life.

In 1963 my husband and I moved to California. Babboo encouraged the move, although she was sad to see us go. Before we left for the long cross-country drive, she gave us a bag of "fun" inexpensive gifts, each wrapped in white tissue paper and tied with a different color of ribbon. There was a gift for each day of our trip. My husband and I were like little kids; we couldn't wait to see what the next package contained. She had enough gifts for a wagon crossing, but we made it in three days.

Within the first year of our relocation to Mill Valley, California, Andad and Babboo came by train to visit. It was wonderful to be with them. While they were visiting I discovered my first banana slug in the front yard of our hillside house. It was huge and exceedingly ugly! Unaccustomed to California "wildlife," I did not like what I saw. Babboo, who obviously had had some experience with slugs, said, "pour salt on it." I ran to the kitchen, grabbed the Morton's box and returned to do the nasty deed. The slug melted before our eyes! (Since then I use Corry's Slug and Snail Bait, but I've never encountered a banana slug as big again in thirty years of gardening in California.)

In the mid sixties Babboo's health began to deteriorate. But that didn't keep her from writing or giving gifts to her family. On December 6, 1964, she wrote me a typical conversational letter. Unfortunately, she also referred to signs her health was not good:

> Where are you? I wonder if you are teaching a great deal. Well you have been so faithful [with corresponding] I can't say a thing. There are 2 boxes from us on the way. Alberta [my aunt] wrapped mine besides shipping for me & Edward & Andad went to Nora to mail them yesterday. Alberta will explain envelopes [cards] which were left out. She will send them with hers. Andad was in such a hurry he packed before

we were ready, so the envelope in her package belongs with the turquoise blue & gold fleur de lis in our box for your birthday.

By the way, do you remember Mrs. Abrams? She nursed you when you came home [as a baby]. She is nursing Mrs. Keller's 1st great grandchild now. Does David know Scott Keller? It is their baby she is nursing. Mrs. A. told Edith Keller [one of Babboo's dearest friends] how dear you were. She said, "Beverly was a perfect doll."

I hope things will arrive all right. I made the list & had to leave selection of gifts to Andad and Alberta. Alberta has been here since her church duties & put on my [back] brace which she does Monday & Sunday. Then she and Edward fix our supper Sunday nights. I feel we accept too many unselfish acts from her & Edward. Edward returned from New York & Philadelphia yesterday. Your Daddy calls every day & comes quite often. Your mother comes with him sometimes.

They want to go someplace Xmas for dinner & I suggested Columbia Club but I find I will not be able to go because of strength & also steps to climb. They have to have more tests at the Laboratory then a consultation with Dr. Wishard as I am not improving as to kidney & they can't find the bug after all the antibiotics they have given me. You can't imagine me this way, but I can't even stand alone, let alone walk.

Father Inness came over to give us Communion the other night & I had a "whirr" in my head . . . all blank & you would have thought I never had taken Communion before. Then I gathered myself together & didn't have a left arm some way. Finally I finished but it was the limit.

In keeping with her humor, however, and not wanting to alarm me, Babboo turned the mention of her ailments into a joke told to her by Father Innis:

A woman went to her doctor's office and as she entered she heard an awful scream from within. Then a nun came out. The woman asked the doctor what he had done or said to the [nun]. He said, " I told her she was pregnant," and the woman was shocked. He then said, "Do you know of a better way to cure hiccoughs than that? It would be somewhat of a shock, wouldn't it?" I doubt if you can read this, but once in awhile a word may come out.

I don't know the nature of Babboo's illness in 1964, but it seems she suffered a minor stroke when the Episcopalian priest was attempting to administer Communion. The brace was for her back, which had been operated on in the fifties as I recall. She was also obviously suffering from a kidney problem, but true to her nature, her sense of humor was intact.

Shortly after Christmas 1964, Babboo learned that she would be a great-grandmother. Her great grandchild, David William Fauvre, was born August 17, 1965. We took Davy back to Indianapolis for the Christmas of 1965. We took the train and it was planned that the Raffensperger family—Babboo and Andad, Ed and Alberta, Bill and Eunice Mae, along with Eunice Mae's parents, Charles and Katherine Howell, would meet our train at Union Station.

Unfortunately, however, our train into Chicago was late, we missed the connection to Indianapolis and had to rent a car. We arrived at my parents' house after midnight, bearing our most special gift, their first grandchild. The next day, all four great-grandparents came over to Bill and Eunice Mae's beautiful new home on North Pennsylvania Street to greet our David William. Putting David into Babboo's arms felt wonderful to me.

It is unusual for a child to be born with all four great-grandparents living. David's were photographed with him by *The Indianapolis Star* and an article accompanied the photograph. It's one of my favorite pictures of all of them. Davy, six months, is wearing his grandfather Raffensperger's christening dress and his great-grandparents were all brimming with love. David William was christened over the holiday in Indianapolis at St. Paul's Episcopal Church. After the service his Raffensperger grandparents held a lovely party for family and friends at their home. It was a special day in our family, a day I will never forget.

We spent Christmas again in Indianapolis in 1966. Davy was now one and a half and able to enjoy toys. Bill and Eunice Mae bought nearly everything they saw in the F.A.O. Schwartz catalog, and I loved watching Babboo and Andad observe Davy with his first toy piano and a little red wooden hobby horse. I wished my grandparents could live forever and be for my son what they had been for me. But, of course, that was not to be.

By 1967 Babboo's health had declined further. In June she started a letter to me in pencil; she finished right before she died. Her letter was written in three segments, over a period of a couple of weeks and I include much of it to show how alert and involved she was with life until the end:

June 24, 1967

Dear Precious:

Of all the dumb things—we are it. This morning when I opened a book I found a little check made out to the Fauvres. I gave the letter I had written to Andad & he didn't see the check which was under the envelope & didn't enclose it. So here it is & I hope you know that Andad & I would not miss you sending an anniversary gift no matter how small.

Oh, how we wished we were out there, taking care of our great-grandson and having the time of our lives. Did your ears burn today? Mildred is here cleaning and needless to say, you were the chief subject & how we all love you. [Mildred Wilson, who cleaned primarily for my parents for many years, was one of my favorite childhood companions.]

Edward & Alberta were here last night a little while & just after they went home, Bill & E.M. came. It was Andad's 83rd birthday & we had a fine evening. Of course, I am not worth much, but we do love our family so much & you know we have to make every minute count.

We received your card and it looks very attractive over there [on a table, perhaps?]. *Maybe this little gift will buy some kitchen utensils . . . Any more news of Tacos?* [Tacos refers to "Taco Bell"; at the time Dave was awaiting news that he and his brother had gotten their first franchise.] *Speaking of utensils—you know I have a lot of Revere & hate it. I just love the stainless steel part but oh, that copper. It is always tarnished.*

Well, I can't manage to write anymore today, but will finish tomorrow.

June 28, 1967

Several tomorrows passed and I couldn't write a scratch, so will try again. It is 11:55 p.m. but I couldn't stay in bed another minute. Received your letter today and have read & reread it. We had not thought of your move to Lake Tahoe, nor of any plans other than Tacos . . . Do try to send some pictures, for we are all off balance now.

The views from your place must be breathtaking [Lake Tahoe condominium] & if I were able, we would be on our way. What does Davy think of it? It sounds like fun for you all to be together, even if a little crowding is necessary. How sweet those babies must be together! [David and his cousins, Lisa and Brad Fauvre.]

The Kothe children were like your three, but there were 5 of us— Eugene was 8 months older than I. I came in here. Then came Emma K, then Katherine B, Louise K. The two families always spent weekends together & it was a circus. Gene [Eugene Kothe] was Captain in the Army of World War I & he & I were closest of pals. He died in Bethesda Hospital, before your Daddy was born, but did live to know Edward. He simply worshipped him . . . Gene always ate at least 3 dinners with us every week & I can see Edward giggle at his antics in entertaining him. It seems that life goes on some way. Well, my history isn't so interesting to other people so had better turn off the switch . . .

What will he do about his garden & what about the master of the garden hose [David, who was 2 and loved the hose] & what about your flower beds? Please tell us all about everything. . . . Time to stop again.

July 6, 1967

Dear Precious. This will be the last installment of this letter, I hope. We have had to have a reunion of the family, but not a happy one, but our family should know how wonderful they are. I had to act up on July 4 with a heart attack & Andad had to call the children. E & A were at Landgrafs [close friends] & he called Daddy & he was wonderful, gentle

. . . & efficient. He & E.M. came after he called the doctors, neither of whom could come (night). Then E & A came & they stayed up with Andad till around 1 o'clock . . . Edward just called to say he had been talking to Dr. R. & since I was not up to going to the office, he was sending a lab technician up for a cardiogram & he would be by later this afternoon. —The cardiogram is over now & suppose the other doctor will come just as Andad starts to eat his supper. This business is no joke.

Must tell you 2 stories on Andad & then I guess I had better terminate this history. You know he & Edward wired my bed, through the floor to the transformer below & I was to buzz it if I needed anyone. I haven't used it lately but he has forgotten & every time I buzz even if he is in your room, he just starts out for the back kitchen door & after he finds no one there, he finally gets back to me.

#2 Edward was putting the lower panel on the Frigidaire—Andad was standing with me just within reach of the door & I was beside him when there was a sharp revolver shot. We turned everywhere but no sign of anything. Next day I talked to Mrs. W. . . . & she asked if I happened to have any canned biscuits in the refrigerator. I had 2 cans & when I investigated—there was one exploded at the . . .

We were up all night watching the temperatures & . . .

Now I must really go. How is "Choo-choo" [David's toy train engine he loved to ride] *Oh, how we would love to see our big boy. Be sure to tell us everything you will be doing or have done & all the news. Everything about pools & beach. Tell Davy Babboo & Andad want to hear all about his activities & Tuffy* [our border collie]. *Did I tell you we had to get a new G.E. dishwasher? Writing by the sentence bewilders one.*

Night

They are taking me to the hospital. Dr. is trying to get 3 nurses. Dr. just gave me a hypodermic. I guess I had better get ready for the ambulance.

Raffensperger Funeral Rites Set For Today

Funeral services for Mrs. Lucy B. Raffensperger, 82 years old, 6845 N. Delaware Street, pianist and clubwoman, will be held at 2:30 p.m. today in St. Paul's Episcopal Church. Burial will be in the Crown Hill Cemetery. Friends may call at Flanner and Buchanan Broad Ripple Mortuary.

Mrs. Raffensperger died Thursday in Methodist Hospital. She was a graduate of the Metropolitan School of Music. She was an officer of the [Day] Nursery Association of Indianapolis and past president of the Butler University Chapter of Phi Delta Theta Mother's Club.

She was a member of the Saturday Afternoon Literary Club, Caroline Scott Harrison Chapter of the Daughters of the American Revolution, and of St. Paul's church and its Dorcas Guild.

Mrs. Raffensperger and her husband, Hiram J. Raffensperger, observed their 60th wedding anniversary April 11. Other survivors include two sons, H. Edward and G. William Raffensperger, and a granddaughter and a great-grandson.

My mother had a strange way of announcing Babboo's death. She phoned us in California and said, "Pack your bags!" For a second I didn't know what she was talking about. Dave and I left David William with his aunt and uncle and flew home to Indianapolis. We arrived in time for the calling hours. I didn't want to see Babboo in the open casket, but Andad was most anxious that I do so. He thought Babboo looked so good, and in a way, she did. Though she had more living to do, I think her letters indicated that she knew her time was drawing to a close.

After viewing this little woman who had so influenced my life through the age of twenty-seven, I broke down in sobs and headed for the restroom where I cried and cried. Dave, as always, was consoling, knowing, as I did, that Babboo's death marked the end of an era, and certainly the end of my childhood. She had loved me unconditionally, spoiled me "rotten," and I adored her.

She was initially buried in the Bauer family plot in Crown Hill, surrounded by her whole family on that summer day. And then she was moved to the plot her son so carefully designed.

Later that summer, Alberta traveled to California with Andad so that he could visit with his great-grandson David. We drove them up to our condo at Lake Tahoe for a couple of days. On the way we stopped at a restaurant near Sacramento which had miniature train. Andad rode the little train with Davy. It was wonderful to see them together, holding hands.

Andad's eyesight had so deteriorated by age eighty-three that he could not live at home alone. His sons and daughters-in-law encouraged him to move into a retirement center near Zionsville. Hoosier Village was new at the time and his apartment was most attractive; my mother saw to that. He was photographed in his apartment for a publicity picture. As always he looked well groomed and handsome. Andad looked and acted much younger than his age, and I don't think he ever left home without putting on a coat and tie!

We visited Andad at Hoosier Village when we returned to Indianapolis for summer trips. He lived to meet his second great-grandchild, Cynthia Elise, born in 1968. Davy called his great-grandfather "The Gumdrop Man," because he had gumdrops in a bowl at his apartment which he always shared with Davy.

As Andad could no longer see well enough to write and had never been the communicator in the family, Ed encouraged him to record messages to us on tape. We sent cassette tapes back and forth between California and Indiana. I have kept those tapes, the small reel-to-reel variety, and gratefully have my grandfather's voice recorded for history. I wish I also had Babboo's.

Andad enjoyed women. He had been particularly fond of his secretary when he served as director of the Ration Board during World War II. He and my grandmother befriended her and visited her and her husband on occasion in Effingham, Illinois. While at Hoosier Village in his eighties, Hiram fell in love with another resident who was confined to a wheelchair. My uncle Ed was furious, but there was no doubt Andad enjoyed her companionship! When she grew more ill and she was moved to the health center, he continued to visit and care for her.

Hiram was the eldest of my four grandparents and survived them all by a few years. He died April 16, 1973 when I was thirty-three.

Hiram Raffensperger, Ex-Merz Officer, Dies

Services for Hiram J. Raffensperger, 88, retired vice-president and treasurer of Merz Engineering Products, will be held at 10 a.m. Wednesday in Crown Hill Gothic Chapel, with burial there. Mr. Raffensperger died yesterday at Hoosier Village, Zionsville.

A lifelong resident of Indianapolis, he was graduated from Emmerich Manual Training High School. In high school he was a member of the varsity track team and basketball team. Following messenger and book-keeping work, Mr. Raffensperger entered the advertising business about 1907. He was a former executive and director of Kothe, Wells, and Bauer Company and was a former president of Ko-We-Ba foods.

He joined Merz about 1943 and remained with the firm until retiring in 1955.

In World War I, Mr. Raffensperger was a member of Company H of the Indiana State Militia. He worked with the Marion County Ration Board during World War II, and later became its director.

Mr. Raffensperger was a former president of the Indianapolis Board of Park Commissioners and a former member of the Hoosier Athletic Club and Meridian Hills Country Club. He was a member of the Columbia Club, York Historical Society, Sons of the American Revolution, and St. Paul's Episcopal Church. He also was a charter member of the Indianapolis Athletic Club.

Friends may call from 2 p.m. to 8 p.m. today in Flanner and Buchanan Broad Ripple Mortuary. Survivors include two sons: H. Edward and G. William Raffensperger, both of Indianapolis.

My father was with Andad when he died. He said he held his hand and Andad's grip was still strong. Dave and I didn't go back for the funeral; I mourned in California. A service was held at the Crown Hill Gothic-style chapel near the cemetery's main entrance. Andad was buried in the new Raffensperger plot on a hill in Crown Hill, next to Babboo, whose remains had been moved there in 1969.

In less than seven years both of his sons would die and join him and Babboo at Crown Hill. The loss was great for this only child and only grandchild.

H. C. Raffensperger Drugstore on the southwest corner of East and South
Streets. Besides dipensing medicines at all hours, Raffensperger Drugs advertised
soda fountains which featured pure fruit syrups.

Hiram Clinton Raffensperger, the druggist who arrived in Indianapolis as a child from York, Pennsylvania.

Anna Losier Raffensperger, the daughter of Joseph Losier, a Swiss immigrant who was killed at the Battle of Shiloh in 1862.

The sons of Hiram and Anna Raffensperger: Burton, Arthur Clinton, and Hiram Joseph, my grandfather.

Ed and Bill enjoy a summer trip to Lake Wawasee, never dreaming they will one day be Naval officers.

The Raffenspergers spent many carefree summer days at the Lilly cottage at Lake Wawasee.

A World War I Bond Drive drew patriotic city people, including German Americans.

Ed saved hotel stickers from the Raffensperger family trip to Europe in 1928.

Ed (at left) looking very Ivy League at Harvard Business School, 1931.

Hiram and Lucy Raffensperger at home on Washington Boulevard, 1930.

Hiram and one of his many fine cars.

Bill Raffensperger around 1930.

Ed's "Dawn Faust" and Lucy Raffensperger.

H. Edward Raffensperger
(1909–1980)

Ed never took a chance on anything.
—A friend

The firstborn child of Hiram and Lucy Raffensperger was their son, Hiram Edward. He was named after his father Hiram, and his mother's maternal grandfather, Edward Branham, but he always used his middle name. Edward inherited not only family names but also the cultural awareness and achievement of four generations of German American ancestors.

Ed was born at the home of his maternal grandparents, George and Lute Bauer, where Hiram and Lucy were then living. His baby book testifies to how much he was welcomed and adored by doting parents and grandparents. As a little boy he exhibited the sense of humor and pleasant nature he would have as an adult.

Ed graduated from Arsenal Technical School in 1926, after showing his interest in business even as a teen by serving on the business committee of the senior play. Sometime during his high school days, the family took a trip to Bermuda. I don't recall if Ed ever returned to this beautiful island, but Bill must have remembered the trip fondly, because he took me to Bermuda when I was a teenager.

Ed received his B.S. in Business Administration from Butler University, Indianapolis, in 1930. He was active at Butler and his scrapbooks indicate that he thoroughly enjoyed his days at the college not far from the family home on Washington Boulevard. He was a member of Phi Delta Theta fraternity and on the student council and served as the business manager of *The Tower*, Butler's literary magazine. Representing the student council, Ed was appointed to supervise the finances of the 1930 "Fairview Follies," an annual variety show. He was treasurer of his senior class and represented the recipients of the Bachelor of Science degree as a commencement speaker. His steady girl-friend at Butler was Alberta Alexander, a Pi Phi.

In 1928 Hiram and Lucy took their sons to Europe for two months, leaving Ed's police dog, "Dawn Faust," in the care of Alberta's family. Alberta's father, Eddie Alexander, was a veterinarian for the State of Indiana.

Europe was a magnificent family experience for the Raffensperger family. It was the first trip abroad for Lucy and Hiram, and I imagine Lucy was looking at Europe from the perspective of her mother and sister's trip twenty-seven years earlier. Hiram recorded it on film while Lucy kept a journal. Ed added European mementos to his college scrapbook. The Raffenspergers left New York for Le Havre in July on a French cruise ship called S.S. *De Grasse* and returned on the Cunard ship *R.M.S. Carmania*.

Ed collected colorful ship and hotel stickers used to decorate and identify luggage and included them in his scrapbook. For a long time I had one of the Raffensperger steamer trunks, covered with those stickers. On the Raffensperger's return to Indianapolis, they entertained Ed's fraternity brothers and their parents by sharing their adventures on film and with Lucy giving an informal talk. A newspaper article, kept by Ed, reported the travel lecture and states that "the family traveled to France, Italy, Switzerland, Germany, Belgium, Holland and England. They traveled by train, automobile, and airplane, as well as by sea."

During their college days the month of May found Ed and his brother Bill working at the Indianapolis Motor Speedway. In 1931 automobile endurance trials were also held at the track. Under the supervision of the American Automobile Association, Marmon Company "Roosevelt" cars broke all existing records for gasoline engines in continuous operation. The cars were driven day and night. Charles Merz and Wilbur Shaw, both race drivers, were the official judges. Ed and his lifelong friends Dave Burns and Mayburn Landgraf were AAA officials. Bill Raffensperger, also an official of the AAA, was the assistant to the official timer, Odis Porter. These four friends also went on a camping trip together one summer during college. They camped close to the Canadian border on an island in Rainey Lake.

Because of a forest fire in the area, Canadian Mounties asked them to leave.

In 1930 Ed entered Harvard Business School's Graduate School of Business Administration. His scrapbooks include his Harvard mid-year and final exams which look quite formidable. Returning from Harvard, Ed went to work for the Eli Lilly pharmaceutical company in Indianapolis. He wanted to be a doctor, but his mother discouraged him. He had been groomed for Lilly.

Ed married Alberta Alexander, his college sweetheart, in October of 1935. The eldest of three girls, Alberta was also born in Indianapolis. Petite and good natured, Alberta adored Ed. And like Ed, Alberta was quick to take on responsibility; she was well-organized and conservative by nature. Both the eldest in their families, they were dependable and always available to their families and friends in time of need.

Ed and Alberta started married life in what had been the home of Aunt Lizzie Bauer, Ed's great aunt, but later moved to a house at 4246 Graceland Avenue. I remember visiting them there and Alberta's baking me cookies. Pictures show Ed and Alberta enjoying summers at a lake, probably Wawasee, with friends, some of whom were from their Butler days: the Landgrafs, Gillioms, Townsends, Burnses, and brother Bill and his wife, Eunice Mae.

Like his parents, Ed loved all kinds of people. As a child, he was introduced to Charles M. Brian on their trips to Lake Wawasee. Dubbed the "Ancient Mariner of Lake Wawasee," Charlie was a colorful character in Syracuse, Indiana, known by most who summered there. Charlie was a traveling salesmen for an Indianapolis millinery firm on South Meridian Street, and had begun his visits to Wawasee as a young man, accompanied by his mother. Devoted to his mother, Charlie never married but after her death he continued to make annual trips to Wawasee in her memory and stayed at "Mrs. Harkless's Silver Beach Hotel," which I imagine became what I remember as just "Harkless's," a boat repair and bait shop on the north side of the lake. An ardent fisherman and sailor, Charlie had a distinctive appearance with his tanned skin, white beard, and naval cap. He boasted that during a sailing race, Colonel Eli Lilly of Indianapolis drafted him as skipper. Ed kept track of Charlie over the years and when he died in Syracuse in 1949, Ed pasted his obituary in his scrapbook.

In 1937 Ed lost his dog Dawn. Registered by the American Kennel Club in 1929, Dawn's certificate of entry into the club shows the breeder as W. E. Stierwalt; the sire was Faust v Stolzenfels, and the dam Queen II of the Hill. On the occasion of Dawn's death, Ed wrote a poem about reuniting with Dawn in heaven. On a special *black* page, he included the poem in his scrapbook along with Dawn's picture.

Though Ed was only twenty-eight when he lost this devoted friend, he never again owned a dog. Instead, as his parents had, he cared for the pets of neighbors and supported the work of the Humane Society. He often walked after dinner, usually with a neighbor's dog at his side. I couldn't understand why Ed never had another dog, maybe because I never knew Dawn. He and Alberta did have a pet canary when they were older, but I always thought Ed deserved another dog.

In 1941 Ed and Alberta went to Florida where they vacationed with his parents, traveling by train on the Pennsylvania R.R. In 1942 Ed received his commission in the U.S. Naval Reserve as a Lieutenant (Junior Grade) in the Supply Corps and was assigned to the Philadelphia Naval Ship Yard. This same year Alberta joined the Auxiliary to the Indianapolis Day Nursery, a volunteer organization to which she devoted many years. She also volunteered for the war effort serving the Red Cross and the Civilian Defense Center.

Despite the fact he couldn't swim and claimed he couldn't learn, my uncle loved ships and the sea. In Philadelphia, Ed directed a staff of eighty-three personnel of the Landing Craft Issuing Group. In a little over a year he was responsible for the loading and shipping of materials sufficient to outfit more than 700 LSTs. Outfitting an LST is something like furnishing a large hotel. Soap powder alone was purchased in amounts of 250 tons.

After Ed's tour of duty as Assistant to the Supply Officer in the Philadelphia Navy Yard, he was sent to the Naval Training and Distribution Center at Camp Peary, Williamsburg, Virginia, for further training in 1945. Later that year he was sent to Manila, the Philippines, via San Francisco and Hawaii.

In 1946 he was promoted as a paymaster to the rank of Lieutenant

Commander and discharged the same year after having served four years. He was fortunate not to see combat and he enjoyed his tour of duty in Philadelphia. I believe he was very proud of his service to his country.

Ed returned to Indianapolis and Eli Lilly and Co., and Alberta taught kindergarten and continued her community service. In 1945 I was one of Alberta's kindergarten students at Miss Cook's, a private kindergarten. She was active with the Caroline Scott Harrison Chapter of the Daughters of the American Revolution, later serving as its president.

Though I am eligible to join the DAR, I chose not to, in support of a stand my father took years ago. He was disappointed in the DAR for denying the black singer Marian Anderson, the first African American to sing with the Metropolitan Opera, the right to sing at one of their national events. I left the DAR to my aunt Alberta.

In 1939 Ed and Alberta left their home on Graceland and moved to 7021 Warwick Road in Arden between North Meridian and College Avenue, where they lived for thirty-one years. It was a small, two-bedroom house. For a number of years, Alberta's mother lived with them, using the front bedroom. Mrs. Alexander, whom I remember as a diminutive woman with gray hair worn in a bun, worked at L. S. Ayres & Co. in the Junior Department, and it was from Mrs. Alexander that I purchased, with some embarrassment, my very first bra.

I remember many good times at Ed and Alberta's Warwick Road home. They hosted many gatherings of family and friends. Despite the smallness of their home, Thanksgiving was always held there, and Alberta was often ably assisted by "Auntie Britz."

Emma Britz, an elderly German woman, had worked for Hiram and Lucy for many years and they had befriended her. She was devoted to the family and they to her. When my grandparents weren't available, she occasionally acted as baby-sitter for me. She didn't drive, so one of the Raffensperger men always had to pick her up and return her to her house south of Thirty-eighth Street on Boulevard Place near Crown Hill Cemetery.

Our family always saved their bacon grease for Auntie Britz. I was told she made soap from it, but I never learned how nor saw the soap.

Auntie Britz was known for her daisy pattern crochet and had made me lovely baby clothes and a bassinet blanket. When I was a little girl she crocheted a matching set for my baby doll. A good cook, her specialty was lemon meringue pie; and our whole family once went to her home to be served this delicious dessert.

When Mrs. Britz became a shut-in in her final years, Ed delivered food trays to her at holiday times. He and Alberta made up trays—Navy issue, stainless steel, as I recall— for any sick friend or elderly person they knew. They both seemed to enjoy doing for others and were natural caregivers.

When I remember my Uncle Ed, I see him sitting in his upholstered chair, feet on the matching ottoman, smoking his ever-present pipe and listening to his police radio, which sat on the mahogany table next to his chair. Ed was a frustrated fireman. The chatter of the police radio never stopped when he was home; he loved "chasing" fires and racing to nearby fires or accidents to see if he could be of help.

One Easter, when I was seven or eight, I accompanied Ed to an accident on the Northside of Indianapolis. A city bus driver had probably fallen asleep at the wheel and run his empty bus into a phone pole. The driver had been removed from the bus by the time we got there, and I watched paramedics attend to his injuries. He was bleeding from the face and head and had a broken arm. Though fascinated to some degree, I was also frightened by all the blood. I couldn't sleep that night and had to be comforted by my father. Ed would have been most upset if he'd known.

Ed managed to get to all the big fires in Indianapolis. When the City Market burned in the fifties, Dave and I were downtown and in a position to view the distant flames from our car. Although the police would not allow us to get closer, I was sure Ed had followed the engines to the site. He had.

I thoroughly enjoyed and loved my Uncle Ed, as I also did my Aunt Alberta. I was disappointed, however, that they didn't provide me with a cousin or two. As an adult and mother, I asked Alberta once why they had never had children. She said it was Ed's choice; she did not mention his reasons. They would have made wonderful parents as both loved children and children loved them.

Sometimes I describe one of the differences I have with my husband—and children for that matter—as "coiled hoses." I coil hoses; however, my husband doesn't see the need. The Raffenspergers kept their hoses coiled, their cars in good repair, and their pantries filled. Their flashlights didn't have dead batteries and all their business papers were in order. Long distance calls were monitored with an egg timer set next to the phone. Like a fireman, Ed kept his home and his office in a state of readiness. I suspect that was a trait inherited from his German American ancestors. Ed even backed his car into a driveway, like a fire engine facing the street, always ready for a fast getaway!

As perhaps best evidenced by Ed, the Raffenspergers had a sense of humor, a subtle fun-loving humor which included a well-meaning practical joke now and then. When Ed and Bill were teenagers and living on Washington Boulevard with their parents and uncle, Clarke Allin, Lucy kept reminding them not to race up and down the stairs of the three-story house. She was concerned they might run into a china cabinet on one of the landings and break its valuables. One day when Lucy was resting on the first floor, the boys, assisted by Clarke, filled a large cloth bag with old glass bottles, and sneaked upstairs. One of them raced downstairs while the other dropped the bag!

Another practical joke occurred the Christmas I was given a chemistry set. This time it was my maternal grandmother who got the teasing. She was concerned that I might get hurt using the chemistry set by myself. Ed and Daddy told her they were taking me down to the basement to help with my first experiment. Once there, they instead lit a firecracker. Everyone else knew of the joke ahead of time so they watched my grandmother, who jumped a foot off her chair!

On the serious side of his life, Ed was dedicated to Eli Lilly and Company, and both he and Alberta were extremely proud of his lifelong affiliation with the highly successful company. Except during World War II, Ed rose early to drive from the Northside of Indianapolis to the Lilly plant on the Southside. Frugal and conservative by nature, Ed often carpooled. He and Alberta had a one-car garage and only one car. My early understanding of Ed's career was observing a decorative glass jar in their bathroom filled with hundreds of empty Eli Lilly capsules of all different colors. It was my favorite item in their home, aside from the dinner bell, which was a four-bar xylophone on an oak base which hung in the kitchen. One Christmas Ed gave me my very own glass jar filled with empty capsules of all colors. I kept it for years.

In high school my class was given a tour of Lilly. I have a strong memory of that tour. My friend Elise Payton Noonan, a fearless soul who jumped horses competitively, fainted at the sight of the cats and dogs being used in research projects. The animals were anesthetized, but were suspended by wires, on their backs, spread-eagled. It was not a pretty sight, certainly not as pretty as the conveyor belts of multi-colored gelatin capsules waiting to be filled with healing powders.

Ed held different positions at Lilly during his many years there but his primary position was administrator of the plant's hospital. When he retired at the age of sixty-five, he was Manager of Industrial Medicine Services. His brother, my father, often said that Ed could and should have done more with his career, but I think Ed was quite content with his work for Lilly.

I wish I could say that Ed and his younger brother remained close and friendly all of their lives. It was not so. They married women of very different personalities and their relationship became more a courteous friendship than a close one. Ed and Bill went in separate directions, both in their careers and during the war. Ultimately, Ed was a cautious man who avoided taking risks, while Bill spent his life risk-taking and making many of his risks pay off handsomely. Ed was safe and stateside in Philadelphia for the most part while Bill experienced firsthand the horrors of war. Ed was proud of Bill's success as an investment banker; he trusted his brother to make investments for him. But Ed didn't understand or appreciate Bill's need to be the best or have the best. He did not share his brother's responsibilities as president of his own company nor his role as a father. He especially did not share Bill's need for power. Ed tried to help his brother when Bill encountered serious difficulties, but he could not.

Ed did not always like Bill's wife, my mother, who was somewhat of a rebel. Eunice Mae, like her husband, wanted both prestige and wealth to buy beautiful things and accomplished these goals. Ed, like his mother, came to partially blame Eunice Mae for my father's problems in life, which I shall detail later. He must have considered his younger brother a paradox; the complexities of my father's life caused Ed pain.

Ed and my father even disagreed on how to care for their beloved parents when they became ill and dependent on their sons. I watched the gradual estrangement between Ed and my father over the years and it saddened me. After my father died, Ed turned away from our side of the family. He never again spoke to my mother and I'm sure he never realized how hard his decision also was on me. He always treated me with the same love and respect, but it was a painful chapter in my life because I knew we were all grieving for my father. I watched my family break and shatter. Every part of my being wanted to put it back together as I had found it and experienced it as a child. But by the seventies, there was not much left to put back together.

The first time I heard the word "cholesterol" was in connection to Ed. In the sixties, he was diagnosed as having very high cholesterol, and I remember he took a small plastic capful of a white liquid with meals. I'm sure it was a Lilly product. Little did I know at the time that he had heart disease. After his retirement he was encouraged to relax and travel to warmer climates during the winter. He chose to return to the sea, and for several years he and Alberta took cruises, returning with wonderful photos of their destinations. When my father died, I looked to Ed to fill his shoes as grandfather to our children. I hoped he would be a grandfather much like my grandfather Raffensperger had been to me. He and Alberta did visit California and our children loved him. Ed loved kids and had a wonderful way with children: non-judgmental, he joked and played. And how could any kid not love a man who loved dogs?

When our son, David William, was born in 1965, Ed sent him an application to join the Navy. He also sent Davy his first Brooks Brothers button-down shirt in a child's size. I suspect he had expectations that this new young man in the family would follow some impressive footsteps. I think he wanted him to know he had an important legacy.

Ed was not able, however, to be the grandfather to my children I had hoped he might be. His heart disease worsened and, sadly, he was not a candidate for surgery. Four years after the death of his younger brother, he too died. He was seventy-one when he collapsed at O'Hare

Airport en route to Hawaii with Alberta. In an action typical of Alberta's thoughtfulness, she took the time to write a thank you to the airport police and paramedics who attended him. In so doing I suspect she was thinking of Ed's lifelong respect and appreciation for those who serve us during emergencies.

Like the rest of his family, Ed had joined St. Paul's, but unlike Alberta and his brother, he wasn't active in the church. He would attend only the 8 A.M. Communion service, saying that he didn't like sermons. A sensitive man, I believe he had a deep inner faith which he chose to keep to himself. When Ed died, so did a part of me, that big part that had been influenced by the three Raffensperger men who had all been vital to my childhood: my grandfather, my Uncle Ed, and my father.

G. William Raffensperger
(1913–1976)

Bill took a chance on everything.
—A friend

My father, Bill Raffensperger, was named after his grandfather George Bauer and his great-great-grandfather William Taylor. His name, George William Raffensperger, was such a mouthful it's no wonder that he first pronounced it, "George Women Waffybodey" and even extended it as a toddler by calling himself "George Women Waffybodey-Big Boy Man-Pat Murphy-Mike O'Brien-Dog-Gone-It!," adding a string of pet names used by his mother and his uncle Clarke Allin. Bill wanted to be a "Big Boy Man"—he wanted to "be somebody." He often said to me, "If you don't blow your own horn, someone will stuff toilet paper in it!" It was important for Bill to know and be known, as had been nearly all his male forbearers in Indianapolis. Consciously or unconsciously, Bill wanted to carry on the German American tradition in his family, the hard work and dedication that resulted in prominence in the community. He wanted to make his mark in Indianapolis. It can be said with certainty that he did.

Like his brother Ed, Bill was born at home in the house of his Bauer grandparents at 2932 North Illinois Street. Bill's birth was complicated. I was fascinated with my grandmother's description of his birth. She described having her ankles tied to the bedposts during what must have been a grueling labor. My father was a twin; however his twin was unexpected, perhaps undeveloped, and was stillborn. The twin was not named and to the best of my knowledge was not buried in the family burial plots.

When Bill was a toddler, the Raffenspergers and Bauers built their large Bavarian-style house on Washington Boulevard. It was there that he grew up enjoying his family and neighbor friend, Dave Burns. Photographs of Bill as a baby and young child show dark hair and gorgeous large brown eyes, his mother's eyes. The pictures also show his intensity: determination is evident on his little face. Babboo said her younger son was also quick to show his serious and sensitive nature.

The Raffenspergers loved to travel with their sons. One of their many trips was to Philadelphia. Billy Raffensperger, eleven, Grade 6A, wrote in 1924 about his visit to the Philadelphia mint and his essay was published in the "Coburn Chronicle," a collection of stories by fellow students:

> *When I visited the United States Mint in Philadelphia, they were making dollars and pennies. An order had just been sent in. We were lucky to be there then because they don't make money very often. A guide took us through a hall with many glass windows looking down on the people making money.*
>
> *First there were blocks of silver and copper about the size of a brick. The blocks of silver were run through rollers until they were the thickness of a dollar. They were then run through machines that cut them into strips the width of a dollar. The strips were afterwards cut into shapes by other machines. The silver shapes were then taken to another room where women put them into stamping machines. In these a pressure of ten tons or more pressed the design into the dollar. After the money was made it was put into banks for safekeeping.*

Money was certainly important to my father, but it was definitely not his only interest. He loved the mysteries of nature and science. Bill was fascinated with butterflies and moths; as a youngster he caught them in a net carefully using chloroform-soaked cotton to kill them. Bill mounted his collection with straight pins, and he studied the different varieties and became rather knowledgeable about the most beautiful of flying insects. As an adult, he still enjoyed looking at them under a microscope, as he did other insects and even drops of blood pricked from his own finger.

Bill was a good student and had an artistic bent. Tribute was paid to his craftsmanship in an article in *The Indianapolis News* on January

30, 1926, written about an exhibit of ship models at the Indianapolis Central Library which read, in part:

> *A vessel attracting more than average interest is a model of the* Santa Maria, *Christopher Columbus' ship built by little Billy Raffensperger, twelve years old, a pupil in School 66. Billy built the* Santa Maria *as a surprise Christmas gift for his mother, and the latter proudly lent the ship to the library for exhibition. The boy's constructive genius, coupled with his imagination makes the* Santa Maria *one of the show things of the exhibit.*

Bill's *Santa Maria* is also shown in a photograph accompanying the article about Indianapolis' model shipbuilders. The *Santa Maria* was donated to the library, but Bill built a second larger ship which was kept in the family. When I was a child, I loved showing my friends the tall ship model my father had carved as a child. It had three or four masts, complete with canvas sails, and a secret compartment in the hold (that was my favorite part!). The ship was displayed on Daddy's workbench in the basement of my childhood home on West Fifty-ninth Street. Eventually he gave it to Eric Eikenberry, a neighbor and news carrier. I hope Eric took good care of it.

Bill did not follow his brother to Arsenal Technical High School. The new Shortridge High School campus had opened on North Meridian Street, much closer to the Raffensperger home. While at Shortridge, Bill was on the Thursday staff of the *Echo*, the daily newspaper, and he ran track one year. As a teenager he became interested in boxing and took boxing lessons from a private instructor, on the third floor of their home. As an adult, Bill enjoyed watching professional boxing on television and even hung a punching bag in our basement.

Summers were spent with short trips to Lake Wawasee in northern Indiana, where the family visited the Lilly family, or on camping trips. Bill was not yet a teen when the family went to Bermuda. He was fifteen the summer the Raffenspergers took their grand tour of Europe.

Despite his fascination with the physical sciences, particularly astronomy, Bill shared Ed's interest in business. He too attended Butler

University, majoring in business administration. And like his older brother, he pledged Phi Delta Theta. In 1932 Butler's Phi Delt chapter was forty-four men strong, including Bill and his Shortridge classmate and close friend, Elbert Gilliom. Bill is mentioned several times in an issue of *The Indiana Gamman*, the newspaper of the Butler Phi Delt Chapter. He was vice-president of the Commerce Club, a member of Men's Union, and on an award-winning bridge team. I suspect his fraternity brothers hoped he'd duplicate the hand he'd been dealt during a game at home in 1931, a perfect bridge hand of thirteen spades! His luck of the draw was even reported in *The Indianapolis News* and mentioned again in a "Looking Backward" column twenty-five years later.

The Phi Delt pins in the thirties were different from those of later years. Bill's pin is special because it has a diamond in the center and is bordered with pearls. When Richard Creveling, son of close family friend Elizabeth Steele Creveling, pledged Phi Delt at Indiana University in about 1983, my mother gave him Daddy's pin.

Bill Raffensperger was a member of the Butler University Men's Glee Club and chairman of the publicity committee for the annual Rose Dance, a dance for freshmen. Memorial Days found him at the track, serving as a scorer for the Indianapolis 500 Mile Race. In 1931 he assisted Odis Porter, official timer, at the endurance trials for Marmon "Roosevelt" cars. Mother also remembered that he drove test cars for oil companies at the track.

It was at Butler University during the fall of his junior year that Bill met Eunice Mae Howell, a freshman. Eunice Mae, a music major and Tri Delt pledge, noticed his picture in the yearbook. Thinking Bill the most handsome upperclassman she had seen, she asked mutual friends, Marge Carr and Al Gilliom, to introduce them. The arranged introduction was made in the fall of 1932, halfway between Eunice Mae's house on Hampton Drive and the Tri Delt house on the Butler Campus. Bill was with his friend Al and Eunice Mae with Marge. Their introduction was the beginning of a long and sometimes difficult love affair.

Eunice Mae Howell was vivacious, talented, and very pretty. In fact, she described herself as one of the prettiest young women in her freshman class, and I wouldn't be surprised if she was right. She thought she might have been named "Freshman Rose" had she been more visible on the Butler campus. Her music classes were at Arthur Jordan downtown.

Eunice Mae was born in 1915 in Beech Grove, several miles south of Indianapolis. As a young girl she lived in Beech Grove and later in Irvington, a suburb of Indianapolis. Her talent for music, particularly the piano, was recognized at an early age and her musical ability was one of the reasons the family moved to the Northside of Indianapolis so that she could attend Shortridge High School and then Butler University's School of Music.

Eunice Mae's family background was considerably different from that of Bill Raffensperger's. She was not of German heritage, her ancestors being English or Welsh and Scotch-Irish. The only child of Charles and Katherine Shockley Howell, her parents were *each* the seventh child in families of eight children.

Eunice Mae's childhood was simple compared to that of her college sweetheart's. She remembered coal oil lamps, outdoor plumbing, and homemade clothes, and as a child she longed for store-bought dresses. She remembered Christmases without toys and a birthday with only a pair of pink anklets for a present, but she traveled a little with her parents because Charles Howell got free rail passes. Her favorite trip was to Pike's Peak.

Her father started working for the New York Central Railroad while still living on the family dairy farm. He would go to work after milking cows at 3 A.M. He also went to high school in Greenwood and Southport. Eunice Mae adored her father and it was easy to understand why. Charles Duty Howell was a most personable, intelligent man whose modesty and sense of humor made him lovable. Eunice Mae shared with her father an aptitude for mathematics and a love of card games. They enjoyed each other's company; Charles Howell doted on his only child.

By the time Eunice Mae and her parents moved from Irvington to Indianapolis, her father was working for the Pennsylvania Railroad and had an office in Union Station. Despite the fact the United States was in the depths of the Depression, Charles made good money, five hundred dollars a month. This allowed the family to build their home in

Indianapolis near Butler University. He was offered a promotion by the Pennsylvania Railroad, but it required a move to Philadelphia. Had he taken the position, it's doubtful my parents would have ever met.

Like Bill Raffensperger, Eunice Mae Howell enjoyed the limelight. At the age of three, she sang "Keep the Home Fires Burning" in front of a patriotic crowd gathered in the Beech Grove Auditorium. Inheriting musical ability from her mother, who could play the piano by ear, Eunice Mae started piano lessons at age six. She studied under June Baker until the eighth grade, when she started attending classes at the Jordan School of Music in Indianapolis. By high school, she was playing the piano in movie theatres and accompanying singers on local radio stations.

Eunice Mae had a sense of independence and ambition not shared by her mother, who was a frugal, cautious woman, content to live modestly. Katherine, or Katie, Howell expressed her creativity through sewing and cooking, with wonderful pies being her specialty. Her husband and daughter taught her to play bridge and she joined a bridge group with other railroad wives. But her daughter wanted more from life and she was quick to experiment with new things.

Eunice Mae and a friend smoked behind their parents' backs and weren't caught until they set a mattress on fire. She learned to sew, made her own doll clothes as a child, and later sewed most of her own clothes, copying the latest fashions. For a Butler dance she painted her nails green. Eunice Mae wanted the love of a sensitive and intelligent man like her father, but she also aspired to be accepted in Indianapolis society and experience a style of living different from her parents'. Bill fulfilled her dream.

Bill graduated from Butler University in 1934 with a B.S. in Business Administration. The same year he served with nine other men on the contest board of the American Automobile Association. He is pictured in a full page advertisement for Conoco's "new and improved germ processed oil" in the May 2, 1934 issue of *The Chicago Daily Tribune*.

Following graduation, Bill began a long career in investment banking. He joined the firm of Schloss Brothers Investment Company in Indianapolis and quickly rose in the firm to Manager of the Trading

Department. Schloss specialized in "local building and loan stocks, Indiana real estate preferred stocks, and real estate mortgage bonds." Schloss later became Morris Plan, a savings and loan company, but by then Bill had his own company.

A chronic strep throat kept Eunice Mae out of school the winter of her college sophomore year. Having missed so many classes, she felt she couldn't catch up and did not return. Bill encouraged her to model, but she started selling hats at L.S. Ayres & Co. Bill proposed marriage and Eunice Mae accepted. Hiram and Lucy Raffensperger welcomed Eunice Mae into the family. It was a family of strong tradition and means which celebrated Christmases with generosity and ceremony. Eunice Mae was overwhelmed when the Raffenspergers gave her a rhinestone bracelet.

Wedding showers and the bridal dinner hosted by the Howells at the Columbia Club were described in the Indianapolis newspapers. It was the beginning of a custom: every major event in the lives of my parents for the next thirty years would be reported in the papers. Bill Raffensperger and Eunice Mae Howell were married February 10, 1935, at the Broadway Methodist Church in Indianapolis. Mother later said she wasn't happy with her wedding gown or the flowers she carried, but I think she looked quite stylish in a long white satin sheath with a train. She carried calla lilies. Ed Raffensperger was his brother's best man and close friend Mary Virginia Robbins served as matron of honor. Following the ceremony, a reception was held at the Raffenspergers' home on Washington Boulevard, and the newlyweds honeymooned in Cincinnati and Asheville, North Carolina.

While Bill was associated with Schloss Brothers, Eunice Mae worked at L.S. Ayres Department Store as a salesperson and personal shopper until her pregnancy in 1939. She admired and sometimes envied the beautiful and often wealthy women she served.

In 1937 Bill decided he wanted to start his own company. Shannon Hughes, a coworker at Schloss Bros., asked if he could join him. They worked well together, each having his own unique style and personality. Raffensperger, Hughes & Co. was formed in January, 1938. *The Indianapolis News* reported on January 3:

Announcement was made today of the formation of Raffensperger, Hughes & Co., Inc., brokers and dealers in investment securities. Active officers of the new corporation are G. William Raffensperger and W. Shannon Hughes. The new investment firm offers a comprehensive investment service to individuals, banks and other institutions, dealing in industrial, public utility and real estate stocks and bonds. Indiana and general market municipal obligations, United States government and territorial bonds also will be handled. Raffensperger and Hughes are well known in the investment business, both having been associated with Schloss Bros. Investment Company for several years. Raffensperger formerly was manager of the securities department of that firm. The new firm has offices at 702 Fletcher Trust building.

This was the era of the Depression, not the easiest of times to start a new business, but John G. Rauch, Sr., encouraged Shannon to join in the venture and served as the attorney who assisted in the incorporation process. A local architect loaned them five thousand dollars to get started and Hiram Raffensperger joined his son and Shannon in signing the incorporation papers. Bill, following in the footsteps of George Bauer, added his name to the commercial community of Indianapolis. A year before the birth of his only child and with the winds of war blowing in Europe, Bill was taking a chance, a chance to become a man of influence and wealth in Indianapolis. He was twenty-five years old.

Bill and Eunice Mae began married life at 245 West Thirty-eighth Street, but soon built their first home, a small white brick house on Sherman Drive in a newly developed area on the Northeast side of Indianapolis called Sylvan Estates. They bought a dog, an English setter, whom they named Judy. At the time their new house was in a semi-remote area, and after Judy was stolen, they began to feel unsafe in the neighborhood.

I was born the day after Christmas, 1939. After two weeks of rest in Coleman Hospital, which was not unusual for the day, Mother brought me home one snowy day in an ambulance provided by her uncle Dick Mussman. The son of the German emigrant Diedrich Mussmann, the first president of the Southside Turners, Uncle Dick owned the Mussman Auto Livery in the El Penn Garage across from the Graylyn Hotel until the mid 1950s. The company leased hearses and ambulances as well as servicing automobiles. One of their mechanics was race driver Maury Rose and the garage was a hangout for the race drivers who stayed at the Graylyn and worked on their race cars stored at the garage.

My father saved the hospital bill which totalled about two hundred and fifty dollars, including phone calls and guest trays. Raffensperger, Hughes & Co. had been in business for a year. Nine months later World War II officially began with Britain and France declaring war on Germany.

Bill and Shannon worked hard at their investment banking business, spending much time on the road. During these early years the corporation was active as a broker-dealer specializing in the underwriting and distribution of municipal bonds. The company history says that Bill figured bids on a Smith-Corona calculator, an easy thing to do at the time since there were only about three different bond coupons. Once my father sold municipal water bonds for the town of Bourbon, an irony he loved joking about. Bill and Eunice Mae sold the white house on Sherman Drive and purchased a two-story red brick and white frame house at 34 west Fifty-ninth Street, which except for the war years would be our home until I was sixteen. The house was only about a mile or two from the Raffensperger's in Crows Nest.

Just as Raffensperger, Hughes & Co. was getting on its feet, the Japanese bombed Pearl Harbor and America entered the war. Although Bill had a wife, a two-year-old daughter, and a young company for which he was responsible, he enlisted along with his brother Ed in the Naval Reserves. Raffensperger, Hughes closed for the war years. He received an ensign's commission and was sent to Naval Officers' Training School at Cornell University, Ithaca, New York. The Fifty-ninth Street house was rented, and Mother and I went to live with her parents, Charles and Katherine Howell, in their home at 314 West Hampton Drive near Butler University. Mother and her sister-in-law Alberta Raffensperger volunteered their services on a Red Cross sewing committee.

Following training at Cornell, Bill was sent to Bethesda, Maryland,

and then Tallahassee, Florida, for further training. Mother and I were able to join him. When my father was stationed in Maryland, I developed a severe ear infection. The local doctor wanted to lance my ear, which could have resulted in permanent hearing loss. Civilian doctors had little access to the new drugs, but the military did. My father was able to reach a Navy doctor he knew who was on maneuvers, and I was given the new and much sought-after sulfa drug. The infection cleared.

During this time, Bill became close friends with fellow Naval officers: Matt Burk whose hometown I don't recall, Fred Nachman from Chicago, Bill Myers from Erie, Pennsylvania, and Jim Gregory from Indianapolis. Bill and Eunice Mae shared housing and some good times with these men and their wives. I was the only child in the group. Eunice Mae enjoyed entertaining fellow officers and their wives by playing the piano at the officers' club.

Bill Myers and his wife Jane remained friends after the war; they traveled to Indianapolis in 1960 for my wedding. Jim Gregory, a career Naval Officer, was Bill's commanding officer in the South Pacific. Forty years later, I discovered his younger sister, Bunnie Gregory Gromeeko, was my neighbor in Saratoga, California! Bunnie remembered her brother talking about my father. He called him "Billy Raff." I doubt my father liked his nickname.

Near the end of 1942, Bill was sent to the South Pacific. He served in Australia and New Guinea for nearly a year. As a lieutenant (junior grade) he was in command of a LCT, a landing craft large enough to transport five tanks and troops. Opportunities to phone home were rare and therefore created great excitement. His letters were censored; only two remain. He photographed the primitive natives of New Guinea who were caught up in a war they didn't understand and those photos, along with those of his fellow shipmates, speak more than words. The Navy men look young, tanned, and are usually stripped to the waist and garlanded with dog tags. There is a sense of camaraderie and dedication in their eyes. The natives, similarly attired, look proud but fearful. Bill sent home souvenirs; many were lost at sea. Grass skirts decorated with shells did arrive for Mother and me. I treasure two souvenirs of my father's South Pacific tour during World War II: a hand-carved wooden comb with long teeth and a white mother-of-pearl pendant also carved around the edge.

Bill's South Pacific tour was difficult. During the long nights he thought about the possibility of death and considered what he would want to tell his daughter if he didn't live to do so in person. At age thirty, my father wrote me the following letter, which is excerpted below:

At Sea—September 24, 1943

To my dearest daughter Beverly—

I had always hoped and prayed that I might guide you and help you all during your childhood and up until you were completely mature and settled. However, if this letter is given you, I will have passed on and have been denied the opportunity to constantly be at your call and give you the advantage of the experience I have been fortunate enough to have had.

"Honor thy Father and Mother"—You have heard that phrase over and over again since you were a child. Beverly, be sure that you do. Mother has made great sacrifices for you and has given up countless hours and days and nights that you might be cared for and comforted, fed and clothed. She risked her very life to bring you into the world and suffered much—all for you. But you can easily repay her by your love for her and your kindness and thoughtfulness to her. Someday you probably will be a mother yourself and probably not until then will you appreciate what this means . . .

You have so much to learn. During the time you are in college make the most of the educational facilities made available to you. In the years to come you will need every bit of knowledge you can obtain . . . If, due to some unforeseen circumstance, you can not attend a university, that should not prohibit you from obtaining a liberal education. Though it will be harder for you to study without direction and without the benefit of the facilities of a university, you can, by applying yourself, read and study much of what would be available at college, merely by reading various text books and works of well known authors and authorities on the subject involved . . .

The main object, it seems to me, is to learn how to live happily and comfortably and yet live a life with a purpose, a life that will not have been wasted. If you marry and raise a family intelligently and success-fully, you certainly could count that as an accomplishment of which you could be proud. However, don't become so completely absorbed in one thing so much that you see or do nothing else . . .

Learn to develop a curiosity about what is around you and you will find so many things of interest that you never possibly could explore them all. Just before I left the country you asked me a question which pleased me greatly. You asked, "Daddy, why does the sun go down?" Though you were only three years old at that time and could hardly be expected to understand astronomy, I explained it you—and gladly. I hope you continue to want to find out the reasons for things happening about you.

When you take a walk through the woods or a garden, avoid merely seeing trees and flowers and birds and insects just as such. If you know something about them you can appreciate them so much more. If you know what a butterfly's wings look like through a microscope, if you know its cycle of life from egg to caterpillar to chrysalis to finally beau-tiful fluttering insect, you will enjoy the sight of one more as it will be far more interesting than just a pretty bug with wings.

Learn to enjoy the simple things of life that are always around you. Learn to enjoy a sunset or sunrise, a fire in a fireplace, a waving field of wheat, beautiful music, a starlit sky. Some of the most pleasant eve-nings Mother and I have had have been before a crackling wood fire in our fireplace listening to quiet, restful music and with the lights low or sometimes just watching the glowing embers in silence.

One of the most awe-inspiring experiences you can have is to gaze into the sky on a clear moonless night when millions of stars are visible, and the infinite universe is displayed before you. When you do, learn to feel the almost terrifying depth and distance of the universe, and appre-ciate the magnificence of it all. Study a little astronomy that you may have at least some comprehension of what you see in the sky. I think that a clear starlit sky is the best church one can attend.

Don't permit your mind to be so preoccupied with the menial, ev-eryday things of life that you can't perceive what is beyond your reach or immediate experience. Study some philosophy—it will help you to learn to be able to break away from the routine lines of thought. But when you do study philosophy, be careful what you believe and remember that most great philosophers were mental gymnasts and logicians and are known for that accomplishment and not for the practical truth of their writings as applied to life.

As for religion, I hope you will always have faith in God and never permit yourself to drift away from Him. Though we can never hope to understand why some things happen the way they do, why good honest innocent people sometimes have the most tragic lives while others who never did a good or helpful deed apparently are the most fortunate, it must be a terrible thing to lose faith. It would seem to me that anyone who does must feel that life is a hollow, shallow, and meaningless thing—and what unhappiness that must cause. To have faith is to live life with meaning and purpose, and in doing so lift it up above a purely animal existence. Having faith will give you strength and courage when you most need it. It will make life fuller and richer and more beautiful for you.

Beverly, when you read this you will be attaining maturity and womanhood . . . As you grow older and begin to think of marriage I hope you choose a husband well. Don't rush into marriage with a young man unless you are sure you not only love him but that you are sure he loves you . . . ask yourself how will he act and treat you under all circumstances, in good fortune and in bad and when the going gets rough (as it surely will sometime in your life) . . . Does he like children and does he want children? Be honest with yourself. Remember it is your own life with which you are gambling—so be sure . . .

Beverly, I apologize for the way this is written. I have had time to put down just a few of my thoughts and hopes and words of advice for you. As I write this it is under trying circumstances. At this moment I am very near the enemy and there is danger—real danger—and the time may be short. I don't know. War is hell—and all of us are being whirled and tossed about in this horrible, chaotic storm. I pray to God that you and Mother may come out of it safely, even if I may not, and that you and she may have happy, beautiful and full lives rich in all the truly good things that I know you both well deserve.

All I ask, Beverly, is that you consider what I have written. I know

you will grow to be a true lady of refinement and intelligence, and be a
daughter of whom your Mother and I could be justly proud.
                                        God bless you,
                                        Daddy

Sixteen years later, in 1959, my father sent me and my fiance a xeroxed copy of his letter. He was having trouble accepting my decision to marry, and I think he wanted me to reread the part about choosing a husband. He needn't have worried, but like any father, particularly such a sensitive father of an only daughter, he did. My father told me in 1959 that when he wrote the letter he thought there was a better than even chance that he would remain permanently at the bottom of the South Pacific because, "As I recall, one sentence was interrupted rather violently by a sneak bombing attack."

Fortunately, my father did not die in the South Pacific, but there is little doubt that the experience changed him forever. Bill survived World War II able to build many a fire in the fireplace, point out the constellations, and share with his daughter the beauty of a Monarch butterfly. He sent me to preparatory school and college, always encouraging me to learn and do the best I could do. He and Mother instilled in me a lifelong appreciation for all kinds of music, and at my father's side I learned the names of flowers and the joy of working in the soil and watching things grow. I never look at a clear night sky without thinking of my father. I studied philosophy in college, which pleased my father, but he was surprised and disappointed with my fascination with existentialism and other non-Christian philosophies. He was sure my professors were leading me down the wrong path; I knew I was just curious, having been presented with new thoughts and ideas, just as my father had hoped I would be.

My father wrote his letter to me in late September. A couple of weeks later, on October 16, 1943, he wrote a cover letter addressed to my mother, which underlined his love and longing for his family:

If this letter is ever given you, Eunice Mae, it will prove that I did
make the worst mistake of my life in entering the service. However, I

did what I thought sincerely was the right thing to do at the time. If I had known what hardships it would bring to you and Beverly, I would have gladly stayed at home no matter what people would have said or thought nor how urgent was the need for men to fight our battle.

One thing I want you to know, Eunice Mae, is that I have always been faithful to you and have always held our love above anything else and it has been the greatest thing in my whole life. I hope that if you should ever remarry that you will always keep a little space in your heart for me and forgive me for the mistake I made.

God bless you and keep you,

I love you with all my heart and soul,

Bill

At the end of 1943, the following article appeared in *The Indianapolis News* :

Lt. Raffensperger Wins Bronze Star for LCT Command

Lieutenant (j.g.) G. William Raffensperger, 31, U.S.N.R., son of Mr. and Mrs. H.J. Raffensperger, Crows' Nest, has received the Bronze Star Medal "for distinguishing himself by heroic and meritorious service in action against the enemy," the Navy department announced.

The citation which accompanied the award said Lieutenant Raffensperger was in command of an LCT in a convoy engaged in the resupply of Arawe, New Britain, December 26, 1943. [New Britain was in 1943 part of the Territory of New Guinea governed by Australia.]

His craft was attacked by thirty-six Japanese dive bombers and fighters. The maneuverability of his LCT was limited, its armament light and, though its vulnerability to such an attack was high, he succeeded in maneuvering his craft during this attack and effectively using all the firepower at his disposal. The citation said further that "the lieutenant assisted in destroying four enemy planes and that, through his efforts, there were no casualties in his command and material damage was kept at a minimum." Lieutenant G. W. Raffensperger is now stationed at Bowie, Md.

I have little memory of the war years, being only three when my father left. Mother and I lived primarily with her parents in Indianapolis where I was loved and well cared for in a makeshift bedroom in an unfinished third story of my grandparents Howell's home on Hampton Drive. I remember playing with the older neighborhood children and hiding under the Howell's dining room table when the adults gathered in the evenings to listen to the news on the radio. I even remember thinking newscaster H. V. Kaltenborn's name very funny. I don't remember the nightmares I reportedly experienced during my father's absence, but I do have a recollection of Mother falling downstairs in her rush to answer an unexpected phone call from my father. I remember Victory gardens and ration books. I wish I remembered more.

When my father returned from the South Pacific, dark-skinned as a New Guinea aborigine, he was a changed man. Family and friends immediately noticed a difference in his personality; even Mother said he was not the man who had left her a year before. Alberta's sister said, "He was shell-shocked, everyone knew it and everyone tried to help him but no one could." Bill had started to drink, heavily at times. Naval officers often consumed more than their fair share of alcohol, especially during wartime, perhaps to pass time, combat fear, frustration, and homesickness. My father also had another excuse for drinking. Toward the end of the war, he was diagnosed with a congenital back problem which often caused him tremendous pain. He explained to me that he had been born with cartilage in his fifth lumbar vertebra instead of bone.

From Bowie, Maryland, Bill was sent to Miami where he was stationed until the end of the war. Housing was scarce, but Mother and I joined him. We first lived in a walk-up apartment near a liquor store and the waterfront. I remember coveting a large cardboard cutout of a liquor bottle, a display I had noticed the store owner carrying. My request was denied. Around the corner past the liquor store was a "gypsy" fortune teller. Her parlor was a tremendous source of fascination for me. One day I sneaked around the corner and peeked in. I still remember my surprise at seeing all the gaily-colored fabrics which curtained the parlor and draped the built-in couch or bed along one wall. Mother grabbed me before I got much further in my exploration, and it wasn't long before we moved.

On the day we left Miami we were an excited and anticipatory family of three. The war was over, and we were going home to Indianapolis to stay. Mother, however, feared we might not make it because a hurricane threatened Miami the day of our departure. At the train station she noted that the flag poles were already swaying, but the train took off and we headed north. We moved back into our home on West Fifty-ninth Street, a united family ready to begin our life again. Uncle Ed returned to Eli Lilly & Co., and Raffensperger, Hughes & Co. resumed business on December 6, 1945. Both *The Indianapolis Star* and *The Indianapolis News* reported the reopening and included photographs of Bill and Shannon:

> *The investment firm of Raffensperger, Hughes & Co., Inc., which discontinued its business in 1942 when G. William Raffensperger, president, was commissioned by the Navy, and W. Shannon Hughes, vice-president and treasurer, joined the Board of Economic Warfare, will resume its securities business tomorrow when offices are opened in the Merchants Bank building.*
>
> *The firm, established in 1937, again will underwrite municipal and corporation securities and deal in general market stocks and bonds.*
>
> *Mr. Raffensperger recently was released to inactive duty in the naval reserve as a lieutenant, after having served three and one-half years in the Navy. He was in the Southwest Pacific amphibious forces and received the Bronze Star.*
>
> *Mr. Hughes, shortly after his appointment to the BEW which later became the Foreign Economic Administration, was made assistant chief of the north and west coast of South America division, whose job was to import strategic materials for the war program and control all exports and lend-lease goods to that area. Early this year Mr. Hughes became assistant chief of the Philippine staff, which position he held until his resignation late last month.*

The late forties were good years for our small family. Our two-bedroom home on Fifty-ninth Street was full of life. Bill and Eunice Mae got to know their neighbors, entertained friends, and my grandparents and aunt and uncle were often at our house. During these years I met Elizabeth Steele, another only child, who lived across the street, and we became fast friends, and I went to kindergarten. In January, 1946, I entered first grade at School 84. That same year I appeared to lose my hearing. My father kept holding his watch up to my ear to see if I could hear; I couldn't, at least not much. The doctors recommended that I have both my tonsils and adenoids removed. After surgery I was returned to a private hospital room. Some of the blood had not been cleaned from my face. My father, the decorated war hero, took one look at me and fainted!

When I became a Brownie Scout meetings were held in our basement. I remember my father drawing a wonderful mural for the wall depicting Brownies at play. He also got neighbors together for informal softball games in the front yard, thereby teaching me the basics of the game.

Our first car after the war was a an ugly gray Hudson. It looked like a box on wheels, certainly not as grand as my grandparents Raffensperger's Cadillac. Mother said the Hudson was delivered with wooden bumpers because chrome was scarce after the war. We were a one-car family until 1956 when I started driving. Daddy took the bus to work in the mornings, and Mother and I would drive downtown and pick him up after work. The trip took about twenty minutes each way, and I spent the time listening to stories on the car radio. My favorite at that hour of the evening was "Straight Arrow."

My father worked hard during the week, often traveling; he also worked over the weekends in the yard. Like his father, Bill loved gardening and had a very green thumb. My father told me on more than one occasion that there were three important things to do in life: plant a tree, write a book, and have a child. He planted many trees: two grew into huge, luxurious maples in our front yard. Eunice Mae preferred indoors activities; she made draperies for both our home and Bill's office; she also sewed clothes, refinished kitchen cabinets, cooked, and played the piano.

Ronnie Woodard, a Shortridge classmate of Shannon's and brother of our family doctor Abe Woodard, joined the firm after the war as vice-president and treasurer. Business was good. In 1948 a business column in *The Indianapolis News* mentioned that "Raffensperger, Hughes & Co., Indianapolis financial house, ranked 69th among the 450 dealers in the nation in securities it underwrote last month; Cities Securities Corp. (another Indianapolis firm) was 85th." Late in 1949 Raffensperger, Hughes & Co. became a member of the Midwest Stock Exchange, enabling the young firm to move toward a general securities business. Certainly my father fulfilled family tradition; Bill Raffensperger *was* somebody.

After the war my father encouraged Mother to resume her study of the piano. She became a student of Saul Bernat, a member of the Indianapolis Symphony Orchestra. For what seemed months, we had not one, but two pianos in our living room for the purpose of practicing a two-piano work for Bernats' annual recital in June, 1948. Eunice Mae and a younger woman named Patricia Burkhead were to conclude the recital with Grieg's Concerto in A Minor for Two Pianos. They practiced forever, or so it seemed to me at age eight. On the night of the recital in the Wilking Auditorium, Mother played second piano during the Allegro Moderato and first piano during the Adagio, Allegro Marcato. The whole family attended the recital, full of pride for Mother's accomplishment. I, however, was stung with embarrassment when Mother momentarily lost her place and had to ask Patricia which page they were on. For the most part, however, they had each memorized their parts and the audience cheered. Bill was most proud of his wife, who like his aunt Katherine Bauer, shared her talent with the community at large. Eunice Mae would often perform for benefit teas and other society functions.

I too was proud of Mother's talent, but more than anything I enjoyed dancing around the living room when she played the latest popular music. Eunice Mae had a friend who worked in the sheet music department at Ayres. As Mother could sight read any kind of music, she would call in her order for the latest hits and soon be playing them for me. We loved show tunes, which we heard on the radio, and anything Gershwin. While my father preferred his wife to play classical music, Eunice Mae played it all.

Business trips often took Bill and Shannon to Chicago and less often to New York and Hartford, Connecticut, where they sold bonds to insurance companies. In 1950 Bill planned a family trip to New England, which may well have been combined with business. We stayed in a lovely resort in Marblehead, Massachusetts. It was my first experience swimming in the ocean. As my mother didn't swim, it was Daddy who took me out into the waves. Mother and I quickly developed a taste for broiled lobster, but we could never share my father's passion for Blue Point oysters.

Nat Hamilton of Smith Barney, Inc., in Chicago was one of Bill and Shannon's business associates. An attractive man, Nat had a charismatic personality and many friends. In May he came to Indianapolis for the 500 Mile Race and included my parents and the Hugheses in his party. For a number of years Nat hosted a pre-race party at the home of his wife's parents, who lived at Fifty-second and North Illinois Streets. My parents loved the Smith Barney pre-race party. At the end of the evening a drawing for cars was held, with those remaining auctioned to the highest bidder. On race morning the same guests gathered again for rice pancakes prepared by George Haskell, another Smith Barney salesman and a gourmet cook. The pancakes were absolutely delicious, dripping with melted butter and maple syrup. Following the pancakes, chartered buses would arrive on Illinois Street to take everyone to the track.

I joined this race group in 1950 when I was ten and loved the excitement. Nat had box seats in the new penthouse section high up in the southwest turn, excellent seats where we could see not only the first turn, but also the straightaway, the start-finish line, and pit row. Nat hired waiters to join his entourage at the race to serve drinks and box lunches of fried chicken. One year he became upset with a waiter who, having no real seat nor a good view, stood at the top of the grandstand next to the portable bar and got smashed. On another occasion, a waiter dumped the water and melting ice from the coolers through the slats in the penthouse flooring soaking the race fans seated beneath us.

In those days, men wore sports jackets and women, dresses, to the race—at least those of us in the box seats did. It was every bit as much a social event as it was "the greatest spectacle in racing." Those were also the years when women were not allowed in the pits nor in Gasoline Alley. Times have definitely changed.

While stationed in Florida my father had met very tall, handsome Robert J. Myers, a native of Cincinnati. Bob Myers, a personable young man and excellent golfer, joined Raffensperger, Hughes as a salesman in 1951. That same year he won the Indiana State Amateur Golf Tournament and was chosen as a golf partner for Bob Hope when he came to Indianapolis to perform at the Indiana State Fair. Because I was too shy myself, my father got Mr. Hope's autograph for me when we joined the small gallery at the Indianapolis Country Club to watch them play. Alluding to Bob's impressive height Bob Hope said, "This is the first time I've ever played with a conning tower!"

Those were good times, most of the time. My parents purchased our first television and we were all fascinated with the black and white images on the small, round screen. I became a fan of Howdy Doody, Kukla, Fran and Ollie, and Hopalong Cassidy. Mother and I loved the movies and frequent trips downtown to L.S. Ayres, which nearly always included lunch at the Ayres Tea Room. Sometimes we saw my father or his business associates having lunch in the adjacent room reserved for men only.

I loved our neighborhood and the friends I made there, especially Elizabeth. We were nearly inseparable, playing make-believe with our dolls, dressing up, roller skating, swimming, and biking. We loved to sleep over at each others' houses, visit Babboo and Andad, and go shopping downtown. We took the bus downtown and I made lists of what we planned to do, which usually included a visit to the toy department of Charles Mayer.

Sometimes Elizabeth and I explored the small attic in my house. To access the attic one had to get into Mother's closet and open a small door. I don't remember any great finds aside from a shiny red electric guitar Mother had bought for my father but which he never learned to play. However, during one of these adventures, I noticed a manuscript with Daddy's name on it. I don't remember the title and I never read it, but I do remember asking my father about it. He said he had written a book once about a man who had a good idea which someone else had stolen and used. It sounded sad and I lost interest at the time. He wrote well, but unfortunately didn't have time to write for pleasure. Now I wonder what happened to that book and if it was somehow autobiographical.

In 1954 Raffensperger, Hughes & Co. was one of the managers forming a nationwide syndicate and underwrote the issue of $280 million-worth of Indiana Toll Road Revenue Bonds. On Sunday morning, December 13, 1953, *The Indianapolis Star* reported:

> *Money market history is being made here. All records for a single financial transaction in Indiana will be smashed this week.*
>
> *The offering of $280,000,000 revenue bonds for building the 156-mile east-west toll road across Northern Indiana is scheduled Thursday in the State House. This is the largest flotation of tax-exempt bonds for 1953 in the United States, second only in all-time standing to the $326,000,000 issue of the Ohio toll Road commission last year.*
>
> *The greatest number of investment houses for a single offering, 487 at last count, form the syndicate prepared to buy the bonds from the Indiana commission and then resell them to investors. Eyes of the world of finance will be on Indianapolis Thursday.*
>
> *Back of this offering for sale of the huge amount of bonds have been long hours of labor by members of the Indiana Toll Road Commission, engineers, attorneys, and financial experts . . .*
>
> *For the sale of the bonds, this management group of investment firms was formed: . . . all with New York, Chicago and other main offices . . . City Securities Corporation, Collett & Co., Indianapolis Bond and Share Corporation and Raffensperger, Hughes & Co., all of Indianapolis. Never before have the Indiana investment houses had such a prominent role in a record transaction of this kind. The group is spokesman for all the 487.*
>
> *The issue is so big that only one nationwide syndicate of investment houses, or brokers can handle it. The bid they make, as to any premium and what interest rate the ultimate purchasers will get, will be determined by the general bond market conditions. The commission may accept or reject the bid.*

Obviously the company was a highly respected success. However, success had begun to take its toll. My father was able to relax a little in his garden, but rarely anywhere else. He drank too much, especially when out with other businessmen. Because of his increasing problem with alcohol, cocktails were rarely served at home or at family gatherings. My father went for long periods of time without drinking, but then might drink heavily for days or weeks, occasionally to the point of hospitalization. When he drank, his personality changed. He became argumentative and even violent as he grew older, often expressing resentments and reliving the pain and frustration he felt during the war.

This was an era when alcohol was almost always an integral part of business and social activities. People had little appreciation of how dangerous its continued and increased consumption could be. Today my father's addiction to alcohol and his painful obsession with the war might well be called post-traumatic stress syndrome, but no one knew anything of that in the fifties and everyone in the family ultimately suffered as a result.

And as for the German American connection it both did and did not exist for this generation of the sons and daughters of the Free-thinkers. After World War II, most of them were just as happy to forget they had any heritage and were just glad to be able to return to peaceful living and making good. Sometimes the burden of "making good" must have been heavy for the families whose impressive businesses had lined our town's main street in 1895.

Control of the Indianapolis Water Company passed out of Indiana when Clarence H. Geist of Philadelphia bought the company in 1912. In 1952 the Murchison brothers, oil tycoons and entrepreneurs from Dallas, Texas, bought all the Indianapolis Water Company common stock held by the Geist Estate in Philadelphia.

The public viewed the Murchison intrusion as something of a personal loss, a collective feeling that part of the old Indianapolis they knew and loved was gone, according to Ed Ziegner, political writer for *The News*. In 1953, a month after purchasing the Water Company, the Murchisons brought popular Scotty Morse, former executive vice-president of the IWC, out of retirement to be the new president. In choosing a local man for the position, citizens had some reassurance that local control and interests would be served. Criticism of the Murchisons, however, didn't start to abate until 1956 when the IWC won their suit in the Indiana Supreme Court to get a rate increase, the first appreciable one since the 1930s.

Morse Reservoir, named for Scotty Morse, was under construction on Cicero and Hinkle Creeks, near Noblesville, in 1954. It was to be Indianapolis' second reservoir. The first reservoir, Geist, was completed in 1943 under the direction of Morse, who was often referred to as "Mr. Water Company." Called an insurance policy against water shortages during times of drought, the seven-billion-gallon reservoir covered fourteen hundred acres of land and was surrounded by thirty-two miles of shoreline.

In 1955 Tom Moses, an attorney who had been connected with Investment Management Corporation of Dallas, an overseeing operation for many of the Murchison interests, was named Scotty Morse's new assistant. When Scotty Morse was named chairman of the Water Company in 1956, Tom Moses was elected president.

That same year, Bill Raffensperger approached the Murchisons and suggested that they sell approximately $2.5 million of their stock to a select group of prominent Indianapolis businessmen. They agreed and the transaction was completed quickly, according to my father, and with tremendous excitement by Raffensperger, Hughes & Co., Inc. The transaction made front-page headline news one evening in April of 1956:

Texans Make Million on Water Stock Sale
Murchisons Retain Practical Control

The Murchisons of Dallas, Tex. have sold 25% of their common stock holdings in the Indianapolis Water Company at a profit which may be close to $1 million. Sale was made "about April 1," according to James D. Clark, Dallas, a major stockholder and an executive assistant to the Murchisons.

Clark refused to disclose the sale price, but the stock has been quoted at about $39 a share. John D. Murchison and Clint Murchison, Jr., who made the sale, bought the stock in 1952 when it was quoted at $18.

The shares sold, which went to unidentified Indianapolis investors, were "about 25% of the stock" held by the two Murchisons, Clark said. It was learned that about 10 Indianapolis residents made the purchase.

Howard J. Lacy II, Indianapolis industrialist and recent president of the Indianapolis Chamber of Commerce, is one of the group that bought the stock. "I believe it is constructive and beneficial for all concerned for Indianapolis people to own a large interest in this important utility which serves our city," Lacy said

Number of shares sold appeared to be more than 47,000. In March the company announced that the two Murchisons owned 94,988 shares each. A quarter of these would be 47,494 shares.

The transaction, which was handled by Raffensperger, Hughes, & Co., Indianapolis investment bankers, would qualify as a capital gains transaction, taxable only at a 25% federal tax rate.

This would represent a net profit of approximately three quarters of a million dollars for the sellers . . .

Clark said the two Murchisons and others associated with them in business now own, all together "not more than 40% of the common stock . . ."

Shortly after the Murchisons bought control in 1952, they and associates and subsidiary companies owned more than 252,000 shares of the 500,000 common stock. Clark told The News that John D. Murchison and Clint Murchison, Jr. were the only stockholders who had sold any of their holdings.

"There is no change in any other stock that any of us own personally," he said, "other than that sold by those two." Clark refused to state what profit was made, other than to say "Yes, we made a profit on it, sure." He said no further sale of stock is contemplated and added that "we wanted to have more representation in Indiana."

The Murchisons' decision to sell a sizeable block of Water Company stock to Indianapolis investors surprised the city. When the sale was publicized in April of 1956, Indianapolis newspapers acknowledged that it was a gesture of goodwill which had returned a majority of the city's water utility's common stock to native hands for the first time since 1912. While the citizens of Indianapolis may have resented the initial intrusion of these Texans known for their incredible wealth and tough business deals, their city was the greater beneficiary. Although the Murchison Brothers still held over 36 percent of the company's common stock, they had unquestionably released 25 percent of their holdings to Hoosier businessmen who were finally identified as: Howard J. Lacy II; William J. Holliday, Sr.; Elbert R. Gilliom; John M. Kitchen; G. Wm. Raffensperger; George A. Kuhn, Sr.; Samuel R. Sutphin; and W. Taylor Wilson. Home rule had been restored.

Howard Lacy was an Indianapolis industrialist and a former president of the Indianapolis Chamber of Commerce. Holliday was a director of Merchants National Bank and Trust Company and a former chairman of W. J. Holliday and Company. Gilliom, a brilliant trial lawyer, was a partner in Gilliom, Armstrong & Gilliom. Kitchen, also a respected attorney, was a partner in Rauch, Chase & Kitchen.

G. William Raffensperger, *The News* and *The Star* and *The Indianapolis Times* went on, had headed the local purchase drive and was president of Raffensperger, Hughes & Company. Kuhn was a partner in Klein & Kuhn. Sutphin was executive vice-president of Beveridge Paper Company, and Wilson was a former president of Wilson Milk Company.

The business editor of *The Indianapolis Times*, Harold H. Hartley, wrote of these men, "There they are. That is the new home team running the water company. There are enough of them around that they will be easy to reach. So if you do not like the flavor of what comes out of the kitchen spigot, you can tell them personally."

John Murchison commented that their purchase increased to 1,750 the number of Hoosiers holding shares in the $40 million utility. Murchison then said, "We are pleased to have this group of Indianapolis businessmen associated with us as stockholders in the water company. Their counsel should be very valuable to the company."

Negotiations with Murchisons required my father to travel to Texas. I remember being disappointed when business trips took him away, but Mother and I loved it when he took us along to Chicago and we stayed in the wonderful Ambassador West Hotel, with its underground tunnel of gift shops connecting it to the Ambassador East. One year Mildred Wilson, the lively and fun-loving cleaning woman who often cared for me, caught a ride with us. Arriving in Chicago, I remember being alarmed as my father drove by the dark brick tenements looking for Mildred's destination. It was one of the first times I had been exposed to poverty, and I didn't want to leave Mildred in the midst of it. My father was sympathetic but also anxious to get his family out of the area.

My father treated black employees well, often taking a personal interest in their lives, but he didn't believe in integration and did not want me attending his high school, Shortridge, which had become integrated in the fifties. As the years passed, however, his views softened.

Around 1947 Raffensperger, Hughes, & Co. had moved from the Merchants Bank Building to the Guaranty Building at 20 North Meridian on the southwest corner of the Circle, the point from which all of Indianapolis radiates. Raffensperger, Hughes, & Co. was and is to this day located on the second floor overlooking the Monument to war dead which dominates the Circle. The company name is still painted in gold neatly on the windows as it was in the fifties, visible but noninstrusive as one looks up from street level. My father took great pride in his office, and I remember his enthusiasm when the company added the sophisticated double wooden entry doors, a beautiful dark walnut conference table, and the teletype which was installed in the sixties.

In the early fifties Bill became associated with Foster-Forbes Glass Co. in Marion, Indiana, which made glass containers such as the bottles for Miller High Life Beer. He and the Fosters became friends as well as business associates. We were invited to join them at their favorite northern Wisconsin lodge one summer. Though it was fun for me, I rode an old horse from the lodge stable who sat down and refused to budge, giving me a lingering fear of horses. Bill and Eunice Mae went fishing with a local guide. Mother caught a muskie and my father shared her excitement.

Another highlight for me of that Wisconsin vacation was experiencing my first awareness of real wealth. One evening after dinner at the lodge, my parents were in the bar where there was a popular slot machine, the first I had ever seen. While they played, I sat just outside on a stairway. An unusually well dressed and coiffed blonde woman stopped to talk with me. I admired her evening bag which she opened and showed me what she had inside: a one-hundred-dollar bill! I had never seen one and was very impressed by her glamour and money in the north woods! My parents later told me that the woman was Mrs. Morton. Whenever I buy a box of Morton's ("When It Rains It Pours") Salt, I think of Mrs. Morton and her hundred-dollar bill.

In 1954 Bill Raffensperger was elected director of Foster-Forbes and became the corporation's investment banker. During the years that followed he arranged the financing of the expansion program of the Marion company through the issuance of both equity and debt securities generating many millions of dollars. As the financial advisor for Foster-Forbes, Bill was employed as a member of the negotiating team which resulted in the merger of Foster-Forbes into National Can Co.

Though many of the families of my school friends left Indianapolis in the summer for their lake homes or extended vacations, we did not. Bill never felt he could take time off from work, so our summers were usually spent in Indianapolis. Mother always said my father didn't enjoy long car trips. I understand now that sitting for long periods of time bothered his back.

Though Bill had trouble breaking away from work, he did want to show his wife and daughter some of the world. He planned exciting trips. One was the spring of 1954, my freshman year in high school, when the three of us traveled to New York City. Daddy took us to "21," and it was at this famous restaurant that I first experienced a steamed artichoke with hollandaise sauce. We then sailed on the small cruise ship, the "Queen of Bermuda," to that beautiful British island for a week. The highlight of the trip was riding the motorized bicycles provided by the hotel and watching the hotel room service waiters balance a tray with one hand while they steered their bikes with the other.

In 1957, the year I graduated from prep school in Indianapolis, the Murchison Brothers decided to sell all of their remaining 250,000 shares of Indianapolis Water Company stock. Bill was selected as their investment broker, and Raffensperger, Hughes & Co. co-managed a nationwide syndicate of investment bankers which offered this stock issue publicly. The stock issue was sold out within a few days.

Subsequently, Bill was elected a director and member of the Executive Committee of the Indianapolis Water Company. He had been instrumental in the hiring of Tom Moses as president of the IWC and they had become friends over the years. Bill very much enjoyed his position on the board. In the early seventies, Tom's daughter, Timmie Moses O'Brien, and I discovered we were next door neighbors in South Harbor on Morse Lake Reservoir. We became good friends as our fathers had. Bill is mentioned and his photograph shown in *Water Runs Downhill*, a history of the Indianapolis Water Company, which includes the biography of Tom Moses and his important contribution not only to the utility, but also to the city of Indianapolis.

Between 1957 and 1971, Raffensperger, Hughes & Co. privately placed $25 million of Indianapolis Water Company First Mortgage Bonds with a number of institutional investors throughout the United States. In 1960 the Water Company decided to develop the land around its two primary reservoirs, Morse near Noblesville and Geist on the northeast side of Indianapolis. Shorewood Corporation, a subsidiary of the Water Company was formed to subdivide and develop the land owned by the Water Company. Bill was asked to be a director of Shorewood Corporation and served on its Board of Directors from 1960 until 1971.

Bill also served on the Board of Directors of 111 Realty Corporation, having been involved in the initial financing of this downtown high rise office and apartment building. 111 Realty was merged into a subsidiary of American Fletcher National Bank & Trust Co. which owned the main banking building.

A regular parishioner of St. Paul's Episcopal Church, which was two blocks from our home on Fifty-ninth Street, Bill was elected to be on the Vestry and served in that capacity for several years. He was also on the Board of Directors of my preparatory school, Tudor Hall School [now Park-Tudor]. He was an active businessman and community servant and he felt good about his involvement. Long a member of the downtown Columbia Club, Bill joined Meridian Hills Country Club in the fifties and played golf occasionally, though golf aggravated his back pain.

Eunice Mae was equally active in the community, involved initially with the Indianapolis Alumnae Chapter of Delta Delta Delta and later with St. Paul's Church (as assistant organist), the Symphony, and St. Margaret's Guild. One year she served as president of the Tudor Hall School parents' association. Though she first found Headmistress I. Hilda Stewart intimidating, they became good friends. Unlike my father, Mother was a real sports enthusiast. She loved basketball and always followed the state high school basketball tournament on the radio from sectionals to finals. She learned to bowl and play golf, becoming rather competitive in both sports. One summer she played in a city tournament and was paired with Jane Nelson, one of the best amateur golfers in Indianapolis. The unexpected pairing made her very anxious, but she and Jane became friends. Eunice Mae opened our home to a young golfer from Seattle when the Women's National Amateur Tournament was held at Meridian Hills Country Club. In the fall of 1956, I shared my room with Anne Quast, who would later go on to win the tournament and became known for many years as one of the best amateur women golfers in the country.

Bill had set out in 1937 to "be somebody" and certainly by now he had exceeded any initial aspirations. Following in the tradition of his grandfather, he had founded his own company as impressive as Ko-We-Ba. He had good reason to be justly proud of his accomplishments, and I know he was, but he was unable to fully enjoy his achievements. To those who knew Bill Raffensperger, especially his devoted family, he was a success; he had carried on the tradition.

Hayes T. O'Brien, who served as legal counsel for Shorewood, remembers Bill as being "a natty dresser." My father did appreciate well-tailored business suits and Countess Mara ties, sharing to some degree Eunice Mae's love of beautiful clothes. He was a short man like his father and brother and rarely carried any extra weight. He did isometric exercises to stay slim and prided himself on being able to walk fast and keep up with taller men. Some said he had a bit of a "Napoleon" complex. Be it clothes, gardens, or the interior design and decoration of their homes, Bill and Eunice Mae had exquisite and expensive tastes. Appearances were important to them, perhaps for different reasons. My father wanted to maintain the tradition of beautiful family homes; for Mother it was a new tradition.

In 1955 Bill and Eunice Mae, with the help of his lifelong friend, David Burns, designed a French Provincial style, one-story brick home on a newly-developed wooded hill not far from the North Crows' Nest home of Hiram and Lucy Raffensperger. Located between Spring Mill Road and West Kessler Boulevard, its address was 6020 Sunset Lane. Bill and Eunice Mae both had definite ideas, each contributing to both the exterior and interior design, as well as the landscaping. They worked with professionals to decorate their Sunset Lane home, but they were very involved, loving the creative process.

We moved into our new home when I was sixteen. It was here in the sixties that Bill came closest to enjoying his financial success. He joined the Indianapolis Orchid Society and had a greenhouse built to raise orchids. He not only raised beautiful orchids of different varieties, but also developed a new strain of cattleya. There were test tubes in the kitchen for months. Bill and Eunice Mae named the orchid for their friend Mary Virginia Robbins. Bill was proud of his orchids, as he should have been, and photographed them when they were in bloom. His framed photographs testify to his talent with this hobby.

That first dream house was a perfect place to entertain and celebrate my grandparents Raffensperger's fiftieth wedding anniversary with a beautiful party hosted by their sons and daughters-in-law in 1957. After the party, Babboo wrote the following letter to her children:

> *Words fail when it comes to expressing our appreciation of the wonderful party our children gave us on our Golden Anniversary. It seems like one beautiful dream now, a dream that will live in our memories as long as we live. Everyone who calls is so enthusiastic about the hospitality and the "fineness" of our children and we are so proud of all of you.*
>
> *Daddy and I have had trouble and sickness and grief and financial worries, but they have been overbalanced by our blessings, so altogether we have lived a well-rounded life and been so blessed in having our wonderful children. God could have given us no greater blessing . . .*

That same year I graduated from the Tudor Hall high school. My parents hosted a party at our house for my classmates, and co-hosted the Class Night Dance at Meridian Hills Country Club. My graduation present was a train trip to California. We traveled across the country, stopping for one night to marvel at the Grand Canyon. Then it was on to Los Angeles. My father liked to do things first class and this trip was no exception. We stayed at the new Beverly Hilton Hotel, where Clark Gable caught Mother's arm when she tripped on a step. We spent a day on the set of the movie, *Enemy Down Under*, and Mother and I took a bus to Anaheim to see for ourselves what this new Disneyland was all about. After touring Los Angeles, we rented a car and drove up the coast to Carmel. On the way, Bill stopped at two orchid farms where he ordered plants to be shipped to Indiana on our return.

In Carmel, we stayed at the Del Monte Lodge on the 17 Mile Drive and played the Pebble Beach golf course with the help of an old caddy, who directed our every shot. Then it was on to San Francisco, where Bill looked up a Navy friend then living in Berkeley. I decided I had made the wrong choice in a college. I loved the University of California. It was a memorable trip.

By this time, however, my father's drinking had begun putting big dents in an otherwise loving and happy family life. Many nights I stayed up, when my mother escaped to their bedroom, and argued with a very inebriated father. Sometimes I too fled and left my boyfriend to cope with my father pounding his fist and raging about the injustices he felt so intensely. His war years were usually the focal point, and I sensed that he felt his sacrifice had not been fully appreciated.

Bill never raised his hand to me, nor verbally abused me as he did my mother at times, but the anger and fear he was experiencing was intense. From the time I was born, family and friends always compared my appearance to that of my father, but when he drank I didn't want to be identified with him in any way. He frightened me and that fear was confusing, because I knew he was also a sensitive, gentle man who loved all living things. A good example of this sensitivity occurred the night our miniature poodle, Misty, caught a bunny in the backyard and nearly chewed it to death. My father brought the torn rabbit inside and covered its wounds with his favorite antiseptic, "Sayman's Salve," a yellow ointment. He put the rabbit in a box, fed it, and when it was restored to good health a few days later, released it in a field.

153

We also had tropical fish because my father loved them. In both my childhood homes we had large tropical fish tanks which my father cared for and enjoyed more than did Mother or I. He liked all varieties of tropical fish, but he most admired angelfish and the colorful betas, the "warrior fish" who fan their dorsal fins when they see their reflections.

In the fall of 1957, after our trip to California, I left for Hollins College near Roanoke, Virginia. As a second-semester freshman, I became so awed by the juniors in my dorm who were returning from a year abroad that I applied for the popular Hollins Abroad program and was accepted. My parents immediately started planning a trip to Europe; my mother had never been and my father hadn't traveled to Europe since 1928. Eventually I decided not to spend a year abroad, but my father still felt a trip to Europe would enhance my education. He and mother asked me join them on the trip they planned for the summer of 1959.

And what a trip my father had planned! We flew Pan Am first class to Paris on one of their first 707s. After two weeks in Paris, we traveled by night train to the French Riviera, where we stayed in Cannes. From France, a private driver took us east through Nice to Monte Carlo and then on to Italy. We visited Portofino, Rome, Florence, and Venice before heading to Lucerne, Switzerland by train. From Switzerland we traveled north through Germany and then on to Austria and Holland. We crossed the channel by air, concluding our two-month adventure in London. It was a most memorable trip filled with first class hotels, private chauffeurs and wonderful tours. Mother's enthusiasm for Western Europe was childlike; she fell in love with anything French. The exchange rate was quite different in 1959, so she bought most anything which appealed; we returned home with antiques and souvenirs I treasure to this day. Bill was happy to share the beauty and history of Europe with his wife and daughter; his drinking recurred occasionally, but most of the time, he was the sober cameraman. Like his father thirty years before, Bill recorded our whole trip on film.

A few months after our return from Europe, Dave and I announced our engagement, hardly a surprise to anyone who had known us as high school sweethearts. Bill wanted to have a wedding to remember for his only child and quickly put his creative wheels in motion. With the exception of our approval of colors and a last minute request for a dance band, Bill and Eunice Mae planned our wedding, sparing no expense. The wedding of Beverly Raffensperger and David Fauvre, children of two old German American Indianapolis families, is still remembered for its flowers. Dave and I were thrilled and Mother later said it was the happiest day of her life.

Babboo adored Dave and remembered his family from her school days. Like the Bauers, the Maus-Fauvre family was connected to the German American community and had made a significant contribution to the development of Indianapolis. Dave's father, Irving Maus Fauvre, was the great-grandson of Caspar Maus the brewer and grandson of entrepreneur Frank Maus Fauvre. The youngest of Frank's six children, Irving, born in 1885, was a young pilot in World War I. As a major in the Army Air Corps and commanding officer of Stout Field, Irving was in charge of civil defense for the city of Indianapolis during World War II. Like his father, Irving studied law and became a prominent attorney in Indianapolis. At the time of his death in 1965, Irving was senior partner in the firm of Fauvre, Dongus, Ging, and Cregor. Civic minded, Irving also served as president of the Board of Aviation at the same time my grandfather, Hiram Raffensperger, also served Mayor Clark as Park Board president. About the time of Dave's and my marriage in 1960, Irving was president of the Indiana Bar Association.

Born in 1905, Dave's mother, Mildred Lorraine Van Allen Clizbe Fauvre, nicknamed "Scottie," was a native of Chicago. A singer and actress, she sang at Lamb's Club events and on her own daily radio program called "Society Notebook" aired by WFBM. As an active member of the Junior League, she toured the Midwest with a marionette show for children. In the forties and early fifties, Scottie also starred in several Civic Theatre productions. WFBM-TV chose her to interview race drivers and other celebrities the first year they telecast 500 Race highlights from the track.

Our wedding and merger of these two families was to be a candlelight ceremony the evening of June 15, 1960, at St. Paul's Episcopal

Church, immediately followed by a garden reception at our home on Sunset Lane. My father quickly made the decision that all the flowers would be orchids. His collection was sufficient to decorate the interior of the house, but not for the church, the bouquets, or the reception tent. Betty Bertermann of Bertermann Bros. was contracted to provide all other orchid arrangements and to decorate the reception tent.

Like her client, Betty was the descendent of one of the early German American families in Indianapolis. Bertermann Floral Co., first located on East Washington Street, was founded by Edward Bertermann around the turn of the century. As a result of all the planning, my father and Betty developed a friendship based on their mutual appreciation for flowers. The reception was catered by the then-popular Mrs. Stacy who provided numerous hors d'oeuvres and an incredible chocolate cake with white spun sugar icing. Waiters served a never-ending supply of champagne. At my request no hard liquor was served, which resulted in a sober and happy father of the bride.

I was twenty in 1960 and would never again live at home. My departure coincided with a decade of difficulties which now began to plague my parents. In January of 1961 Bill was sent to the Mayo Clinic in Rochester, Minnesota, for a spinal fusion. He was drinking heavily. Mother strongly wanted me to accompany them; however, I was in the midst of final exams and didn't want to leave college and my new husband. My mother even phoned Herman Wells, then president of Indiana University, who had a business acquaintanceship with my father. Not expecting his call, I was taken aback when the president of my university introduced himself to me on the phone and gave me permission to postpone my exams. Nevertheless, I remained at school and kept in touch with Mother by phone. My father's recuperation was lengthy.

By April of 1961 he and Mother were happy to share their lovely home with the public. The G. William Raffensperger home was featured on the Park School House and Garden Tour, and *The Indianapolis Star* gave the house a full-page spread in the society section:

The French Provincial house is the epitome of elegance. From the black and white foyer to the gold and white kitchen, every detail has been carefully worked out, even to the proper antique finishing of candelabra and fireplace equipment.

Two years ago the Raffenspergers went to Europe and selected many of the things that now grace their home. Fabrics and paintings were found in Italy, sconces, candelabra, urns and curio cabinets in France, and other fabrics in England. All have been skillfully blended to give a lived-in look.

The formal living room and dining room are in white and gold and beiges with touches of blue. In the spruce-paneled family room are evidences of two family hobbies: Mrs. Raffensperger's console organ and the planter in the bay window, a place to display the rare orchids her husband raises.

The house was designed by David V. Burns, AIA. Mrs. Dora Ogden, AID, was the decorator. Landscaping was done by Frits Loonsten.

In June of that year, after completing my student teaching, I graduated from Indiana University. Much to my disappointment, my father was still recuperating from his surgery, which proved to be only partially successful. He was unable to make the trip to Bloomington for the graduation ceremony. He did, however, send me a letter of congratulations, excerpted below:

June 5, 1961

Dear Beverly,

Upon the occasion of your graduation and the acquisition of a Bachelor of Arts degree, and not having written you a letter of serious mean since the year 1943, I realize now it would be appropriate to put in writing my congratulations for your achievement . . .

Beverly, the education you have obtained from the professors and facilities of the colleges and universities in which you have studied should not be considered by you more than a preparatory course nor anything but a prelude to the knowledge and education attainable by experience.

You now have the background and have studied the minds, thoughts, and deeds of notable men and women who have lived during the historical past. I believe that you are now intellectually inquisitive which is a most desirable trait . . .

Knowledge by itself is relatively useless. Knowledge used unwisely is destructive; if it is used wisely, great benefits may be bestowed upon mankind. Those individuals who are able, educated, and who have been gifted bear great responsibility to those less fortunate. The teachings of Christ (of which you are aware) are specific. One who is more able than others must tend those less able—the greater one's ability the greater the responsibility.

With love, Daddy

As I reread this letter today, I am struck with the tenor of his words as contrasted to his 1943 letter he referred to and which I cherished. These letters illustrate two important changes in my father over the intervening eighteen years: his emotional withdrawal and his obsession with work. Somewhere during my childhood Bill Raffensperger had begun distancing himself from those he loved, rededicating himself almost solely to his career. I recall that it was around this time that my father confided in me that he hated weekends. Bill was intellectually stimulated by his work: it also served as a distraction from his physical and mental pain. And then, of course, there was more temptation to drink on weekends. He had by now begun to feel the tremendous responsibility of maintaining his success and it was becoming a burden.

My husband David received his MBA that same year and Bill offered him a job as a salesman with Raffensperger, Hughes. Irving Fauvre, Dave's father, discouraged his son from accepting the offer until he had proven himself in the business environment. Dave went to work instead for IBM. Bill was very disappointed and felt Dave had made a mistake, but Dave had not. An ill wind had begun to blow into my father's business even though Raffensperger, Hughes was still operating a most viable investment firm and my parents were continuing to live very well on Sunset Lane.

In the winter of 1962 while teaching junior high school on Hanna Avenue on the Southside of Indianapolis I mysteriously contracted infectious hepatitis, which was misdiagnosed as flu. I was hospitalized at the old St. Vincent's on Fall Creek for a month. My large private room and bath, complete with a big tub, cost thirty-five dollars per day! My father approached my husband and me and offered to give us a generous down payment for a house. We had been renting and were not yet in a financial position to purchase a home. As my parents assured us there were "no strings attached," we gratefully accepted the offer. We purchased a new house on Melbourne Road while I was still hospitalized. Mother supervised the move during a snowstorm.

A tragic event and bizarre portent of the future occurred at Christmas, 1962. While attending Christmas Eve services at St. Paul's together, we saw my father and uncle's longtime friend, attorney, and fraternity brother, Elbert Gilliom, in the congregation. The day after Christmas, television and newspapers reported that Elbert had been found dead on the street in front of his office building. My family was stunned. Gilliom's death was front page news, and it was initially believed he had been killed by a hit-and-run driver in the early hours of the morning. The first news reports were wrong. Having been diagnosed with a serious illness, Al had taken his own life, jumping from the Consolidated Building on North Pennsylvania Street.

My parents' lifelong friend—who, along with his wife, had introduced them—was gone. Since their days together at Butler both Al and Bill had both become very well known in Indianapolis. The son of a former Indiana attorney general, Gilliom was vice-president of the Indiana State Bar Association at the time of his death. He also served on the School Board and was vice-chancellor of the Episcopal diocese of Indianapolis. During World War II he served as an FBI agent. Each successful in their chosen careers, these fraternity brothers both gave fully to their city, their church, and their country. When Al died, Ed and Bill Raffensperger lost a loyal and valuable friend.

After enjoying our new home on Melbourne Road on the northwest side of Indianapolis for a year and a half, Dave and I decided to

move to San Francisco to enjoy the warmer winters and the companionship of Dave's older brother, Chuck, and his wife, Jinny. Dave was
granted a transfer by IBM. Bill and Eunice Mae were most disappointed
with our decision, and it began to become clear that their gift had been
an enticement to remain in Indianapolis. Despite their arguments
against our move, we sold the house, packed up and drove West. My
grandparents supported our decision; my parents didn't even say goodbye.

The Christmas of 1963 was our first in California. Bill and Eunice
Mae attempted to forgive us for leaving our childhood home and flew
out for the holiday, showering us with Christmas presents and deco-
rations which they had fun purchasing in San Francisco for our Mill
Valley home across the Bay. Both my parents, however, seemed tired
and tense. We encouraged them to extend their vacation and take a
trip to Hawaii, where Mother had never been. To our surprise they
liked the idea. Unfortunately, the Islands brought back memories of
World War II, which affected both my father's mood and behavior.
Their trip ended badly when my father drank too much on the return
flight and was asked not to reboard the plane in Los Angeles.

Not long after this, my parents separated briefly. Bill was troubled
but unwilling to accept help and my mother felt frustrated and unable
to deal with his alcoholism. She moved into an apartment, but their
separation didn't last long. My father was lonely and miserable without her. Before long, they reunited by selling their home and moving
into a new apartment building at Fortieth and North Meridian Streets.

When they could work on a project together, such as decorating a
new residence, Bill and Eunice Mae were a wonderfully creative team.
Their apartment was attractive with their furnishings and the addition of parquet floors. They were happy for a while. Initially, neither
seemed to miss the responsibilities of a large house and yard, but it
wasn't long before the novelty of apartment living grew old. They
found a lot in a newly developed section of old Williams Creek and
bought the property at Seventy-second and North Pennsylvania. Once
again the Raffenspergers decided to build a dream house.

My father designed a French townhouse of limestone. A magnificent home, it was very much influenced by the formal French style

they had so admired in Europe in 1959. The open foyer included a winding staircase to an upstairs guestroom and bath. The living room was 20 by 20 feet, and the dining room large enough to seat twelve. Each room had teakwood parquet floors of a different pattern. The baths were elegant, marble with gorgeous Sherle Wagner fixtures. Mother's bath had a sunken Roman tub of ivory marble and Daddy's bath was a rich, deep green marble. The furnishings were Louis XVI. Gorgeous silks, damasks, and velvets were not only used for draperies and upholstery, but also as wall coverings in some rooms. They purchased antiques and those bought in Europe in 1959 shone as if the house were designed with them in mind. The Aubusson carpet lay in front of the fireplace and the Swiss clock and matching candlesticks sat on the mantle. Though the library was a warm green and the living room had red and blue accents, the primary feeling was definitely white and gold. From my point of view the overall impression was elegant affluence—beautiful, but not comfortable.

Even the gardens were formal, much more so than on Sunset Lane, but there was no greenhouse; Daddy no longer raised orchids. Though exquisite and once again a testimonial to their expensive tastes, I felt the house was ostentatious and impractical for their needs. A New York decorator had been hired, but it was their choices which determined the direction. They loved their creation and took pride in their French home which symbolized their financial success and status in the community. Like their home on Sunset Lane, the Pennsylvania Street townhouse was included on a house and garden tour. They also played host to one special guest, John Murchison. Mother was very excited to have the opportunity to have a man of such national reputation spend the night in the gorgeous guest suite on the second floor. Under her critical eye, the guest quarters were picture perfect for his arrival. Murchison, however, proved a disappointment to Eunice Mae, who had undoubtedly projected onto this Texas tycoon quite a different persona than what she experienced. She said he was as common as "an old shoe," or something to that effect. His brown suit was baggy and unpressed and he left a hair-oil spot on the elegantly upholstered headboard.

The Christmas of 1965 Dave and I took our six-month old son back to Indianapolis to meet his grandparents and great-grandparents and to be christened at St. Paul's, as I mentioned earlier. We took the train and missed our connection in Chicago. We rented a car and drove to Indianapolis, arriving about one in the morning. The new maternal grandparents were up and waiting, Daddy dressed and freshly shaved to greet his grandson for the first time. Self-conscious about his heavy beard, Bill didn't want to risk scratching his baby grandson's face!

Young David was photographed by *The Indianapolis Star*, surrounded by his four great-grandparents in the French-style living room of his grandparents' home. Bill and Eunice Mae hosted a lovely reception at their home after the christening. It was a very special day.

The following year, 1966, we again traveled to Indianapolis for Christmas and my parents held a magnificent Christmas party for neighbors, business associates, and even some of our friends. The guest list of nearly one hundred included the Frank E. McKinneys and the James J. Saxons. Mr. McKinney was the president of the American Fletcher National Bank and a neighbor; Mr. Saxon was visiting from Washington, D.C., where he held a financial position with the government. My parents were excited they could both attend. Their home was perfectly designed for such parties, although my parents rarely entertained anymore.

"Mother" Raffensperger, Bill's devoted mother and my Babboo, died the summer of 1967. Mother told me that Daddy literally threw money around the emergency room of Methodist Hospital when Babboo, near death, was brought in by ambulance. His grief and frustration at what he imagined was the inattention of the medical staff was more than he could bear.

I saw little of my parents over the next couple of years. My father didn't enjoy trips to California. I was busy caring for a two-year-old as well as helping to design and build a new house in Saratoga, where we had relocated. Early in 1968 I became pregnant with our second child. My father's back continued to cause him ongoing pain at this time and pain killers were prescribed. Unfortunately this medication added to his problems.

It was not then properly understood how addictive painkillers could become, nor how deadly if combined with other drugs, particularly alcohol. During these two years, my father was hospitalized as a result of combining prescription drugs and alcohol. His medical crises began to take their toll on my mother as well. Eventually, however, his strength and determination prevailed and he was back at work full-time.

In 1970 Raffensperger, Hughes & Co. purchased a large number of bonds to resell, a common practice. To fund the purchase of this inventory, Bill and Shannon borrowed heavily from the Indiana National Bank. Soon after the company had acquired the bonds, the Federal Reserve, in an effort to dampen inflation, raised interest rates. This single, simple action spelled the doom of Raffensperger, Hughes & Co., Inc. As interest rates increased, the value of the bonds declined proportionately to the point that the bonds could not be sold for as much as my father's firm had paid for them. The end result was that the bank foreclosed on the loan.

Nothing Bill nor his partner could do was able to salvage their life's work or personal savings. The bank took control and arrangements were made for the company's sale to Unified Underwriters, Inc. The partners of nearly thirty-five years were ruined, but their company was not. L. Gene Tanner, who had been hired in 1958 and who at that time had broken ground for over-the-counter equity trading, became the new president.

Shannon Hughes was quite different from Bill in many ways. He was warm and personable and did not suffer from the driven intensity of my father nor his personal problems. Shannon's strength lay in negotiating with the large New York companies, enjoying the entertaining required. Like Bill he was extremely proud of the success of Raffensperger, Hughes and had devoted his life to building the investment company to a place of prominence in the city and Midwest. He was so devastated by their loss that he attempted suicide. His life was saved, but his career was over. Though he tried for a while, he would not work again in the Indianapolis business community.

In 1971 Bill was forced to resign as an officer and director of Raffensperger, Hughes. He was briefly named vice-chairman of the Board of the new Raffensperger, Hughes & Co., but the title meant little. He was now a mere sales representative of the company he had founded and led for more than a quarter of a century. Bill was not only humiliated, he was unhappy with the new ownership and the changes made in large and small matters such as the new contemporary design of the company letterhead. The new officers initially changed the company letterhead from Raffensperger, Hughes & Co., Inc. to simply R, H & Co. My father's self-esteem was increasingly weakened by this reversal of his life's path, but being the stubborn and tenacious man he'd always been, he didn't give up. Not yet.

Bill and Eunice Mae listed their luxurious French home with a realtor. They moved into a small but attractive new home in the College Park development off West Eighty-sixth Street. Though their budget was slimmer, they again joined forces to decorate their new residence cheerfully. Bill Raffensperger, now fifty-eight, considered changing jobs. A friend even suggested he might teach at his alma mater, Butler University. He wrote a most impressive and professional resume, but in reality he found he lacked the energy or motivation to begin a new career. He remained a sales representative.

Between 1970 and 1976 my parents moved four times, back and forth across the far Northside of Indianapolis. First it was the College Park house, then a larger house, whose address I don't even recall, built into a hillside in a nice development on the northeast side of the city. This home was a poor choice. The yard was so steep my father could not mow the grass or enjoy gardening. Hiram Raffensperger was settled in a retirement community several miles west, an inconvenient distance to visit. Bill again started drinking heavily. At times he terrified Mother with his unrestrained anger.

Their next move was back to College Park, which was much closer to Andad Raffensperger at the Hoosier Village Retirement Center. This home was an attractive split-level house, and once more Bill and Eunice Mae eased their pain by decorating the home smartly. The furnishings were still primarily those of the Pennsylvania Street house but somehow they still looked welcoming in this less formal setting. Mother made a new friend in College Park, a younger woman closer to my age than hers and who shared her enthusiasm for interior decorating. Eunice Mae enjoyed the energy and interests of younger women, often finding that she had more in common with them than with her own peer group.

By 1973 all my grandparents had died. My parents' fragile lives had been further stressed with the problems and grief associated first with the Howells' illnesses and then that of Hiram Raffensperger. About this time my husband Dave and I learned from my father of the planned Shorewood development around Morse Lake in Noblesville. During our summer visit to Indiana we bought a lot on Mulberry Circle in South Harbour for a small summer home. Bill and Eunice Mac were excited that we would once again be Hoosiers, if only for the summer months, and they would have the opportunity to know their grandchildren better. And they did for a while.

Bill's grandson David William celebrated his eighth birthday at South Harbour. We rented the clubhouse for a small party and my parents attended. Much to everyone's surprise, Granddaddy Bill stripped to his swimming trunks and dove into the pool with the kids! He was sixty years old, and though it must have been years since Bill had been in the ocean or a pool, he hadn't forgotten how to swim.

Around this time my parents moved again, this time to a white brick ranch on Woodbridge Lane just north of Ninety-first Street between Springmill and Ditch Roads. Again, using their sense of creativity and good taste, my parents added unique and personal touches to the home. And again, though they could ill afford it, they used the services of a decorator to enhance the house with beautiful window coverings and wallpapers. It was well built, most comfortable, and a conveniently located home, a house like so many of the others which they might have enjoyed for the rest of their lives.

Fourth of July had always been a time for getting together with family. When I was a child we had often gone to the Butler Bowl to see the fireworks. On Sunset Lane, Mother and Daddy would buy aged strip steaks and invite the family for a picnic. Daddy charcoaled the steaks in his beautiful back yard while Mother prepared corn on the cob. Babboo brought her famous fresh tomato, green pepper, and onion salad. My then-boyfriend Dave would come, and so did my Uncle Ed and Aunt Alberta. In the style of the German ancestors of old, we would shoot off firecrackers and spin sparklers and have fun. I always loved that day with its patriotic flags, the fireworks, and my family around me.

The South Harbor Home Owners Association had a family-oriented Fourth of July celebration starting with a parade of home-decorated bicycles. Our children participated in 1974 and 1975. Bill and Eunice Mae would drive out to Noblesville for the parade. I remember my father's Fourth of July outfit one year. He looked handsome in a navy and white checked sports jacket and dark red slacks. We again anticipated their annual visit on the Fourth of July of our Bicentennial Year, 1976. But things were to be different.

We should have seen the signs. The last time Dave and I had visited with my father, shortly after our return that summer, we had had a serious and lengthy conversation wherein Bill Raffensperger reviewed many aspects of his life. He was tense and nervous, having only recently accepted his alcoholism and the tenets of Alcoholics Anonymous. He reminded us of the successes in his life and his generosity. He concluded by asking if he could borrow some money from us. Though we were aware that my parents were now spending their money cautiously, we had no idea they were in financial distress. Bill didn't ask his thirty-eight-year-old son-in-law for any specific amount, so Dave wrote a check for about the same amount his father-in-law had given us in 1962. My father seemed grateful, but not enthusiastic. He looked and acted like the depressed man he had become. We were saddened, shocked, and concerned.

Bill had not admitted his alcoholism until thirty years after World War II. To finally admit that he was alcoholic was, I imagine, an admission of failure and weakness, neither of which was acceptable to my proud and sensitive father, who carried the family heritage and expectations like a cross. AA had come too late; his spirit was broken.

Mother, however, was enthusiastic about her new job selling designer fabrics out of their home for a St. Louis company. She had started selling dress fabric like the then-new ultrasuede to local seamstresses, and she made beautifully-tailored coats and suits of the ultrasuede she purchased for herself.

That Fourth of July morning, as I was preparing and cooking for the big day, my father called. He said he and mother had had a disagreement about what he was going to wear and they were not coming out. He sounded disappointed and tired. I tried to change his mind and said they were welcome if and whenever they decided to come.

We had included another couple in that year's celebration. They had just arrived and introductions were being made with our children when the phone rang. I answered and heard my Mother crying and saying something like, "Your father's in the car and he has hurt himself." It took Dave and me twenty minutes to reach their home. While we didn't know what to expect, we shared a horrible intuition.

My husband and I were greeted at my parents' door by a couple, whom I later learned was Daddy's AA sponsor and his wife, who told us my father was dead. I was directed to my mother's bedroom, where I found her in shock and crying. Dave went to the garage to identify my father's body and confirm to the police that my father was right-handed and that a handwritten note found in his car was indeed in his handwriting.

My father had directed his last words to my mother, his wife of forty-one years. He wrote

> *I have done this for I cannot and will not drag you down with me. My mind has been confused for several years and even during the last year and a quarter of sobriety I have made so many errors of judgment that I fear for my sanity.*
>
> *It would be unbearable for you and me for me to be put in an asylum. I have prayed to God for guidance and for him to tell me what to do. This is the only answer that comes back to me. I love you as well as Beverly so much it is impossible for me to ruin your life.*
>
> *All avenues to the solutions to our problems seem closed to me. There is no hope for me to remove the terrible burdens placed on your shoulders except by my action. All our assets and insurance should take care of you with Beverly and Dave's help.*
>
> *May God forgive me for what I am about to do. It seems that all the accomplishments that I could do have been done in the past. In the past few years I have tried so hard but without success. I believe that God is telling me what to do and this is to give up my life so that you, Eunice Mae, a far worthier person, may live. You have so much to*

contribute to society and have happiness again without the burden of me to carry, an impossible task.

It is with these thoughts that I must go now. Jesus Christ, our Lord, I repent for all my sins. I love you, Eunice Mae, with all my heart and all my soul. If I am forgiven I pray that we shall be together again in heaven.

I am desperate for I see no way out of our financial problems except this. My life insurance should take care of all our debts and then some.

Bill

His last letter reminds me of the final lines of his congratulatory letter to me upon my college graduation when he wrote: "the greater one's ability the greater the responsibility." But Bill had taken his sense of responsibility much too far. By 1976 my father could no longer fight his internal war. Depressed and hopeless, he chose to sacrifice himself for what he thought would be his wife's welfare. Perhaps he remembered his close friends, Elbert Gilliom and Shannon Hughes. They too had found life too painful to bear. They too had wanted to spare their families what they imagined would be a burden.

Sometimes I think suicide had long been in the mind of my father. For many years he had contemplated and prepared for death. He purchased a small silver cross with which he wanted to be buried. Before his casket was closed I added another cross, the crucifix from the Jesus Tree. At the time it seemed right.

Shortly after my father's funeral, which was held at St. Paul's Episcopal Church and attended by many old friends and the Indianapolis business community, we learned for the first time that a personal bank loan had been due July 5. Neither Dave nor I had any real knowledge of the extent of my parents' financial situation. It was sobering.

The night of my father's death, Bicentennial fireworks brightened the sky above Indianapolis and an air of celebration was everywhere but where we were. At one point as I heard the explosions, I thought of my father and almost felt I could hear him say, "Remember, I went out with a bang!" On the two-hundredth birthday of the nation for which he gave his soul, if not his life, my father raised a gun and killed the pain which had tormented him for so long. As much as I grieved, part of me understood. Since that night almost twenty years ago Orion has come to be a symbol for me of the strength, faith, and courage he believed in. I look at that constellation as my father must also have on good nights and bad and I remember him.

As I said earlier, my father told me many times that there were three important things everyone should do in a lifetime: plant a tree, write a book and have a child. He did them all; yet like his German American forebears he did much more. Pride in self and family was very important to the German American, but earning that pride often cost dearly. That my father achieved so much despite the weight of the responsibilities he felt and his own human weakness is a tribute to both the strength of the man and the German American tradition.

My father often teased me about having a poor memory. There are, however, times one never forgets: these were such times.

> *And the times that we remember, are the times we can't forget*
> *Like the sparrow in the winter all we need is hope*
> *And the news of today, is the same as yesterday . . .*
> *People struggle, people fight, to find out who they are . . .*

—From "Spin," lyrics and music by David William Fauvre

Epilogue

Bill and Eunice Mae were married for forty-one years. Life was hard for Eunice Mae after Bill's death, but there were some good times and she survived him by seventeen years. During those years Mother and I came to know and appreciate each other as we never had before. Eunice Mae, who became "Granny," not Babboo, to her grandchildren shared her longtime enthusiasm for sports with her son-in-law, her musical knowledge with her grandson, and her passion for fashionable clothes and sense of humor with her granddaughter, a third-generation Tri Delt.

Mother was always young at heart and in appearance. An avid IU basketball and Atlanta Braves fan, Mother was up-to-date on all the sporting news. Though she wasn't enthusiastic about her college-age grandson's long hair and earring (wishing he had the clean-cut looks of a Steve Alford or Damon Bailey), she absolutely adored Andre Agassi!

She lived alone and was lonely at times, but took pleasure in knitting and cooking, visiting us in California for the holidays, and enjoying the friendship of a devoted friend, Edith Hamilton. She sold Leiter's designer fabrics and then worked briefly at L. S. Ayres and as a receptionist at Canterbury Beauty Salon. Her last position was as a telemarketer. In her late sixties she underwent successful surgery for both uterine and breast cancer within a period of a year showing tremendous courage and a positive spirit.

One Fourth of July we surprised her with a new car decorated with red, white, and blue balloons. When she could no longer manage the steps in her two-story condo, we purchased her a new, one-story condo which she enjoyed decorating and found most comfortable until her health forced her to move eight months before she died. My mother didn't like to talk about the difficult times of her life, and she possessed an inner strength and resiliency which never ceased to amaze me. She died in 1993 at age seventy-eight from complications from emphysema, surrounded by many of her favorite furnishings and pictures, those she had shared with Bill Raffensperger.

Shannon Hughes suffered a stoke in 1974 and his devoted wife Marianne helped care for him for the rest of his life. Marianne currently works as an assistant to attorney John G. Rauch, Jr. Barbara, Shannon and Marianne's only child, served as the flower girl in my wedding in 1960. Mother and I attended Barbara Hughes' wedding twenty years later. It felt so good to see Shannon proudly walk Barbara down the aisle of Christ Church Cathedral on Monument Circle. Married to a clinical psychologist, Barbara Hughes Erard is a practicing attorney in Detroit and the mother of two sons. Shannon died in 1988 after a long illness.

Raffensperger, Hughes & Co. was sold by Unified Underwriters to Evan Lilly Noyes, Jr., in 1975. The great-great-grandson of Colonel Eli Lilly, Noyes acquired the firm as an investment. Gene Tanner continued to direct the day-to-day business. As far as I know, Bill remained as a sales representative until the time of his death in 1976.

At this writing, the fifty-seven-year-old investment company is strong and well, its headquarters still in the Guaranty Building. Under Noyes' ownership the firm expanded and opened branches throughout Indiana. The firm's capital grew from half a million dollars in 1975 to $5.5 million in 1986 when Raffensperger, Hughes was acquired by the Associated Group, Inc. Since that time the company has continued to expand its branch office network and opened the first out-of-state branch in Michigan. For these past twenty years, I have felt a sense of pride when I looked up at the gold lettering on the second floor windows and could see my father's name. Though his company had passed into other hands, his company name remained, and that fact helped me accept his loss. In the beginning it was a two-man firm. Today there are approximately two hundred employees!

While writing this book I learned that Raffensperger, Hughes has been sold to National City Bank of Ohio and its name will be changed to National City Investments. Life ultimately teaches us that nothing ever stays the same.

Eunice Mae Howell as a young girl.

Eunice Mae in her bridal gown in February, 1935.

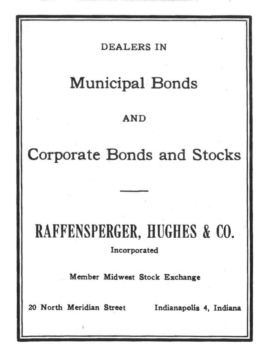

DEALERS IN

Municipal Bonds

AND

Corporate Bonds and Stocks

RAFFENSPERGER, HUGHES & CO.

Incorporated

Member Midwest Stock Exchange

20 North Meridian Street   Indianapolis 4, Indiana

Bill Raffensperger and Shannon Hughes, former employees of Schloss Brothers, form their own company while still in their twenties. World War II forced them to shut the doors while each served his country.

Bill at work in the office of Raffensperger, Hughes & Co., 702 Fletcher Trust
Building.

Lieutenant G. William Raffensperger.
Bill served in USNR from 1941–1945.

Eunice Mae and daughter Beverly in matching pink pinafores.

Eunice Mae and Beverly posing on the wall of Cincinnati friends Mel and Mary Virginia Robbins.

Bill and Navy friend Bill Myer, from Erie, Pennsylvania, relaxing at home while stationed in Bowie, Maryland, circa 1944.

Bill Raffensperger photographed the aborigines of New Guinea, whose lives were caught up in a war they didn't understand, 1943.

Always a handsome couple, Bill and Eunice Mae attended a postwar reunion party of fellow Naval officers and their wives in Chicago about 1946. Everyone looks young, hopeful and so happy. The war is over.

Childhood friends Dave Burns and Bill Raffensperger with their daughters, Nancy and Beverly, 1945.

Indiana Orchid Society members Goldie Wheeler and Goethe Link are shown Bill's greenhouse by Eunice Mae at a party in 1958.

Bill, Eunice Mae, and Beverly on the Queen Elizabeth I returning from two months in Europe, the summer of 1959.

Geist, Morse to Be Luxury House Areas

Picture on Page 12.

By CHARLES VAUGHAN, Business Editor

Plans for one of the largest waterfront real estate developments in the Midwest were announced today by the Indianapolis Water Co.

Geist and Morse Reservoirs are included in a plan to develop the picturesque, timber-studded acreage into a suburban luxury community that will include a private country club.

Geist, however, has immediate priority and its 2,782 acres of land will be used for more than 1,800 homes on sites ranging from slightly less than 1 acre to 4 acres or more.

As soon as it is practical, it is planned to develop the surplus land at Morse according to the needs of the time and depending on growth of the area.

Preliminary surveys at Geist have been completed and sites are now available for inspection by prospective purchasers.

Other projects envisioned for the area, to be known as Shorewood, include a large marina, a number of small private marinas, a community shopping center and a private country club.

A wholly-owned subsidiary

of the water company has been formed to handle the development program. Designated the Shorewood Corp., it is headed by C. Harvey Bradley, former president of the W. J. Holliday Steel Co. here.

RECREATION ON LAKES UNAFFECTED

Thomas W. Moses, president of the water company, stressed that there will be no change in recreational activities on the two huge lakes.

There are no plans to change the present use of Geist by boats of the County Line Dock or the Indianapolis Sailing Club, since sailing and small boats would continue to be the predominant form of boating on the reservoir.

However, bank fishing in the area between County Line Road and the dam will be discontinued because of the development project. Moses said adequate provisions for bank fishing will be made upstream from County Line Road.

Present picnic areas will be relocated apart from the residential areas. These also will be improved with convenient access from Oil Well Road or 116th Street.

Bradley's organization will operate as an independent company. In the early stages, however, it will utilize office

space and share some of the personnel of the utility.

Atkinson & Co. will develop the first section of Shorewood. This section has 184 lots on approximately 250 acres on the north side of the reservoir.

Kenneth L. Schellie & Associates will act as planning consultants to the Shorewood Corp.

Preparation of the land, including grading, road construction and utilities installation, will begin as soon as weather permits. Warren M. Atkinson, head of the development firm, said some lots may be ready for sale and construction by June or earlier.

Atkinson said 2,541 acres will be platted into lots, while the balance of the land will be used for 40 miles of road. A total of 435 waterfront lots will occupy 950 acres and 1,431 "inland lots," adjoining scenic malls, will cover 1,590 acres.

As one feature of the proposed development, the lands now occupied by the County Line Docks and extending southwest along the Sailing Club area are being reserved eventually for a water-oriented luxury apartment. It is expected that the installation will contain a distinctive restaurant and specialty shops.

Lake Home Areas

News coverage of Geist and Morse Reservoirs being opened for development by the Shorewood Corporation.

Bill Raffensperger, Tom Moses, and Daniel Morse.

'Punch' Lines

The Indianapolis Star

Listening Post

Sunday, May 1, 1966—Indiana Sesquicentennial Year

HOOSIER HABITAT

Kitchen Tour Begins To Take In Entire Houses

McDERMOND HOUSE PRESENTS ELEGANT SIMPLICITY
Remarkable Strength Characteristic Of Haute Epoque Style

EVERY DETAIL PRECISE AND PERFECT
G. William Raffensperger House Has Architectural Symmetry And Significance

By Mary Waldon
Home Furnishings Editor

FRIDAY the 13th may be a jinx for some, but to those working on the Kitchen Tour it is a good omen.

It is the opening day of the tour and its 13th anniversary as well. The tour man have been born under the protection of a lucky star for the weather always has been just right.

Committees have functioned with the expertise of a space missile launching crew, and crowds have been so pleased with the tour that they have multiplied like the Biblical loaves and fishes.

THE KITCHEN TOUR IS SPONSORED by the Women's Society of Christian Service of Meridian Street Methodist Church. Mrs. Joseph W. Ferree is chairman of arrangements.

It may sound like instant success to have a house tour for about 600 people with luncheon served at noon in the church but that isn't the true story.

There is the endless detail that goes on for a year preceding each tour. Houses are carefully selected for variety, distinguished architecture and decorating.

Parking problems are considered, insurance taken out, tickets printed, maps drawn and hostesses briefed.

Good Samaritans come through with unexpected favors like Fred J. Grumme, executive vice-president of Aero Mayflower Transit Company, who knows that protective runners for homes on the tour are needed and has had them delivered to a central location for the committee for the last five years.

Kitchens have been the main attraction ever since Mrs. Carl Watson conceived the idea and was chairman of the first tour but little by little more rooms have been added until it has become almost a complete house tour.

One of the most exquisite houses to be seen is the formal French Chateau that has recently been completed by the G. William Raffenspergers at 7920 North Pennsylvania Street.

The Raffenspergers took pictures of a similar chateau on one of their European trips and the perfection and detail in their translation is rich and splendid.

THE ALL-AMERICAN HOME OF THE John P. Holtons at 155 Forest Boulevard is an inviting place that is a gracious mixture of contemporary with some of the charm of New Orleans and a hint of Colonial. No particular effort has been made to achieve formal symmetry or dazzling composition but it has the unaffected aura of relaxation and present-day realism.

American comfort is combined with informal French Normandy architecture in the home of Mr. and Mrs. Maurice C. McDermond at 432 Forest Boulevard. Everything has been kept simple and classic. Colors and woodwork are light and the house has a marvelous feeling of space. Textures and harmony play a quiet role in the uncomplicated home.

Other houses on the tour are the homes of Mr. and Mrs. Fred C. Tucker, 6141 Sunset Lane; Mr. and Mrs. Norbert F. Schaefer Jr., 840 Spring Mill Road and Mr. and Mrs. John P. Main, 728 East 58th Street.

(Related Story and Pictures on Page 4)

Star Photos
By
William A. Oates

KITCHEN LOOKS IMPORTANT WITH FORMAL WINDOW TREATMENT
Raffensperger Kitchen Has Natural Cupboards With Bristol Blue Trim

DEEP REDS IN McDERMOND DEN
Return To Past In Modern Interpretation

HOLTON STONE HOUSE HAS CONCERN FOR ELEGANCE
American Contemporary Preserves Comfort And Stability

HOLTON LIVING ROOM EMPLOYS SLATE BLUE
Quest For Comfort Is Evident In Low-Seated Chairs

FORMAL GARDEN IS SEEN THROUGH WINDOW
Colors In Raffensperger Drawing Room Are Blue, Garnet And Cream

Officers of Raffensperger, Hughes & Co., confer with client John Foster in the conference room of the investment firm. From left: Robert J. Myers, vice-president; Ronald B. Woodard, vice-president and treasurer; G. Wm. Raffensperger, president; John M. Foster, president of Foster-Glass Company, Marion, Indiana; and W. Shannon Hughes, executive vice-president, 1959.

David William Fauvre in Granddaddy Bill's christening dress looks up at his four great-grandparents Charles and Katherine Howell and Lucy and Hiram Raffensperger, December of 1965 in the Pennsylvania Street townhouse of proud grandparents, Bill and Eunice Mae.

34 West Fifty-ninth Street . . .

1943 . . .

. . . and 1995.

Crown Hill Cemetery, Indianapolis 1995.

A Romance in Fourteen Letters
by
Lucy B. B. Bauer

New York Seminary
Oct. 20th 19___

My dear, dear Mother,

How strange it seems to be away off here, and separated from you! I can hardly realize it yet, and until I do, cannot complain of homesickness, nor indeed any other feeling than a sort of dazed wonder at myself, Virginia Taylor, transplanted from my southern home in my namesake state to a suburb of this busy city.

I like the appearance of things greatly, and all seem so sincere in their work. The seminary is beautifully located, on a high point of ground, and surrounded by trees. The lawn slopes gradually to a beautiful little stream which they dignify by the name of river, but which is to me hardly more than a creek. My room is on the top floor, and in one corner. Rather my rooms, for I have my bedroom and studio adjoining.

I have a lovely toned piano, and when I am not teaching, am at liberty to practice all I care to, having no other duties, excepting at mealtime and when we go for a walk. Then I have charge of nearly two dozen girls.

Imagine me a chaperon! I know your're laughing now, Mother dear, you who have always chaperoned me wherever I went, but your must get used to my new dignity, and learn to think of your daughter as a humdrum music teacher in a girls' seminary, instead of the brilliant artist we once fondly dreamed of. How we did plan for my going abroad to study the piano, and become famous! I could almost see myself going out upon the concert stage, a celebrated artist, a vast audience before me, with your dear face shining

183

out from among the others, a bright, particular star of encouragement and, amid the applause which greeted my efforts, your smile of approval should count for more than all the rest.

Those were great hopes, little Mother, and I believe I could have risen equal to the occasion, having satisfied the demands that would have been made upon me; but God willed otherwise. The money we counted on was all swept away, and we had to be content.

So, let us rest here, thankful that my knowledge and experience had gone far enough before the crash came, so that I am able to say conscienciously that I am a good pianist and have a gift of teaching what I know. You have enough to live on comfortably, and I am earning more than enough for my needs, so we're rich yet, Mother, don't you see?

When you write to me, don't neglect to tell me everything that happens in the dear old berg. Come out of yourself, and be a real gossip for my sake. I want to keep in touch with all at home, and while I shall not have time for much correspondence, I would welcome letters from any of my friends, and write when I could. To you I shall write more regularly, as you will expect reports occasionally.

I have not told you enough about my new quarters. My bedroom is cosy, with south windows. I have a bed, dressing-table, chiffonier, center table, two straight chairs and a comfortable rocker. I shall not tell you how these are arranged, for by the time this reaches you, they may be in some other position. You know my penchant for moving things around, which I inherited from a certain little woman I know.

Do you remember Father's once saying it would not be safe for him to retire in the dark, as he would be apt to go to bed on the dresser, if you had done the cleaning that day? My room lacks pictures, but that can easily be remedied the first time I go to the city.

Of course, I have not been to New York yet, but am looking forward to the time, and consider myself lucky to be so near the metropolis, where I can hear all the great artists, and feast on music whenever my duties here will permit.

But I am off my subject again, and must hurry this letter along. My studio has south and west windows, and some musicians' pictures hang in groups around the wall. They are all of old masters, with one exception. He was, or is, a violinist, no one seems to know who; but I am sure he sunk into oblivion from sheer lack of brains, for he had his picture taken while in the act of playing on the G string, and is peeping up over his fist like he was afraid to let the whole glory of his countenance shine on you at once. I shall do away with him as soon as I can get something else (I should have said some other thing) to put into the frame.

Besides the pictures my studio contains piano, desk, table, chairs and a couch. Now, do you not think me well fixed?

Suppose I was over in Germany, stuck off in some little 2-by-4 room, with no such comforts, and working hard to win the approval of some gruff old professor. It is better as it is, Mother dear, and we'll be happy over it, will we not?

Write soon, for I expect your letters to be the bright spots in my life, and the more spots the better for

> Your loving daughter,
> Virginia

✣

A___, Va. , Oct. 25th 19__

My dear, brave little daughter,

How happy I am that your first report should be so cheerful, and tell of such comfortable surroundings!

My little girl has a way of looking at the bright side of things, and I hope she may always be able to do so. Our own natures make our lives, to a certain extent, and I have always found that there is no situation utterly hopeless.

My own tendency has been to look for the ridiculous in life, and although I have often overstepped the mark, (once I laughed at a funeral), I have found that to be able to look on the funny side, is to be able to see the sunny side.

A Sunday School teacher of my youth once requested each girl in her class to bring a text or motto from the Scriptures that she thought she could live up to, and adopt it as her life guide. My selection was: "A merry heart doeth good like a medicine, but a broken sprit dryeth the bones."

I have always been able to believe, at least, in my text, and by trying to live up to it, have missed many a spell of blues it forbade me to have.

We are all living in the same old rut here. Nothing startling has happened, unless it be a visitor who is among us, whom you should remember as an old playmate. Surely you can recall Nora Smith? She had a brother Mack, and you three were always together. You know they left here when they were about half grown, and we have never heard of them since. Nora says they went abroad and traveled quite extensively. Upon their return, they settled down in Washington, all but her brother, who was so in love with Europe that he remained there.

She asked particularly for you, and was disappointed not to see you. Says she will hunt you up when she goes to New York, which she will do in the near future. She is a very handsome, stylish girl, so you will not be ashamed of your visitor when she comes.

Yes, I had a good laugh at your being a chaperon, yet I know these girls will be safe in your hands, as you have always been so consciencious in your home life, that I can trust you to be sufficiently dignified when occasion demands.

But, dear child, do not cultivate stiffness, for I should then imagine that your disappointment, which is one of the great sorrows of my life, had changed your bright, sunny nature, and that I could not bear.

While I am denied the pleasure of seeing you among the great artists of your chosen profession, surely God willed best, and the reason for it will come to us later.

Your friends all wish to be remembered to you, and rejoice with me that you are so nicely situated.

I am content that there are no boys at the school, for I am always afraid some one will come along and steal the heart of my Virginia from her selfish old loving

Mother

N. Y. Seminary, Nov. 12th 19__

Dear little Mother,

I am writing this while I rest from a long day in the city with six of our big girls. They had, or thought they had, some shopping to do; and, while there was not a sensible thing, and surely not a necessary one bought by the whole bunch, it gave them a day of pleasure and change.

Your own girl was not slow to enjoy it also, for I don't want to forget that I am only twenty, and some of my charges are within a few months of it.

What a big place New York is! Yet we didn't get lost, and no one took us for greenhorns; for one of the girls, Miss Ella Adams, has always lived there, so we had a guide.

I did not need anything for myself, thanks to your thoughtful care in selecting my wardrobe; so my only purchase was a lovely picture of Elsa Rugger, the cellist we heard last winter, which I have already transferred to the frame which contained my peeping violinist. Now,

I can look in the direction of that picture without feeling like I want to hit somebody.

In my last few notes, I have kept you pretty well posted in regard to the workings of this school, and the part I take in its busy life. I am doing so well with my pupils, and feel as though maybe this is my calling, after all.

I have had a visit from Nora Smith, and indeed you were right in saying she is a handsome girl. She created quite a stir among us. I was surprised to see her so soon, and indeed I should never have known her.

As luck would have it, she came on my leisure day, so we had the whole afternoon for a chat about old times. How we did laugh about the fights her brother Mack and I used to have! And what a little peace maker she was! But once I broke his heart entirely, and she never was quite able to smooth that over.

You see it was this way: I had been talking of going abroad to study when I should be older, and Mack, who thought he had a voice, said: "I am going to be a great singer some day. Maybe I'll go abroad too."

I well remember how I laughed at him, and told him in no very ladylike words that he had no more voice than a rabbit, and that anyone by the name of Mack Smith would never set the world on fire as an artist.

It seems he never forgave that, but it may have been the best thing that could have happened, for you know that everyone who can sing to suit the audience in a Sunday School exhibition does not satisfy the leading critics of the world, by any means.

Nora says Mack is doing a fine business in Europe, through several countries, so I think he owed it to my good advice that he is not a little one-horse singer in a concert company somewhere.

Speaking of singers reminds me: Our vocal professor has at last arrived. Herr Schmidt is his name. He really is a fine singer, and a perfect little gentleman; but I must describe him: Most of the hair he has is in his name, for there is not a spear of it on top of his head. He is small and wiry, has sharp black eyes, a pointed nose, the least mite of a mustache and a tiny mouth.

These features all combine to give him the appearance of a rat, and I always wish he would sing behind a screen, so I couldn't see him. We all like him, so far, and I am glad to accompany him in his music, which work of mine he compliments highly, saying he never had a better accompanist.

I have discovered a genius! Not a pianist, but with such a voice! It is a wonder. I had noticed for sometime that a girl across the hall seemed so interested in my music. I have surprised her, listening at the door when I practiced; so, as that was no crime, I invited her to come in when she cared to. She seemed so happy at the permission, that I asked her if she played at all.

"Oh, I do so love music!" she answered, " but my music comes from my throat."

I wondered why she was not studying, and asked her. Poor child burst out crying and said, " Oh! if I only I could! But Grandmother has forbidden me to be a musician, and declares no money of hers shall ever go to music of any kind. I do sing a little, only what I have picked up myself, for no one ever taught me."

I persuaded her to try a little favorite of mine, while I played for her, and her lovely voice thrilled me through and through, untrained as it was. What might it not be with proper guidance! I asked her if her parents lived.

"My mother is dead, " she answered," and my Father dead to me."

Of course I did not question farther, but found her name to be Irene Roberts. The last name, by the way, being that of her grandparents, and not truly her own.

There is a sorrowful mystery somewhere, and I imagine it to be con-

nected with music in some way, else why would the Grandmother be so bitter? I am wondering what to do about her, for I know I could help her, but I want your sanction first.

Think of it, Mother dear. This girl, so gifted, yet denied the power to cultivate that gift. Would it be wrong for me to teach her the little bit I learned from Madame about voice culture?

I await your answer eagerly, and shall take no steps in the matter until I hear from you. Stretch your conscience a little, Dear Heart, for my sake, for you know God did not give her that voice to waste. I could start her in the right way, and trust to the future for her. She is just eighteen, the right age to begin training. You always know best what to do, so please advise.

Your loving daughter
Virginia

✿

A___ Va., Nov. 20th 19__

My dear girl,

Your letter came as usual, to welcoming hands. I am always glad when one of your "reports" rolls around. You had made a home for yourself at the Seminary, a thing you would do anywhere, if you had half encouragement.

I was glad to know that Nora called on you, and laughed with you over old times. Poor Mack! How could you be so ugly to him? He was quite a favorite of mine, but I am glad, since he is a successful business man, that you headed him off from what might have been a mistaken career.

I enjoyed your description of the Professor, and laughed heartily over it, though of course you know not to describe him to any one else. Poor man! It is not his own fault, and if he is gentlemanly and the artist you say he is, just look on the side, and forget his appearance.

I must write now, of your little friend with the big voice, as I know you are anxious for my opinion. I look at it in this way: If the girl is so passionately fond of music, and has such a voice, not all the grandmothers in the world could keep her from using this talent for her own pleasure.

The only question is: Shall she be allowed to use it in an uneducated, wrong way, or shall it be guided in the right direction? I say the latter, and if my little girl can help her, I am glad to have her do so.

The grandmother may think she has good reason for what she does, and we do not know the circumstances. I am glad we do not, for then we might hesitate to take a hand in the matter. As it is, you find this young girl, hungering for something within your power to give, and you give it as you would bread to a person starving. I hope to hear much from the pleasure you both will get from this arrangement.

So you were complimented upon your accompaniments? It is not the first time, as you know and I think it a good gift.

I don't know but I am glad of the rat-like countenance of the music-master, for I am still dreading the time when the " man of all men" shall appear for you. When he comes, Virginia, do not let all my foolish twaddle keep me out of your confidence; but put off his coming as long as possible.

I hope, before many months to be counting the days until I see you.

It is too far for you to make me a Christmas visit, but I shall make time fly in every possible way until spring, then it will not be so long.

I am going to Grandfather's for the holidays, as I should be lonesome here without my little girl, and a sorry Christmas I should spend. You, I feel, will be happier, knowing I am not alone, and you'll have your girl friends, and a merry holiday, I hope.

It is early in the winter to be thinking of the nice long summer we will have together, yet I find myself already planning different pleasures for that time. Oh, well! It keeps my foolish old brain busy, and castle building was always a great hobby with me.

I am preparing a Christmas box for you, and shall send it early, but if it reaches you too soon, do not open it until Christmas morning, for I wish to greet you in my own way on the day of days.

Your young friends are so attentive to me that I feel quite elated. I am asked to chaperone on almost every occasion, and they insist that "Mother Taylor's house" shall be headquarters, just as though Virginia were here.

I know they have written to you, so, of course, you are kept posted about all their gayeties.

And now I am sleepy, so goodbye for another time. I have just enough "wake" left in me to sign myself

Your loving Mother.

❄❄❄

N.Y. Seminary Dec. 25th 19___

Dear, darling Mother,

No wonder you wanted me to keep my box unopened until Christmas morning! When I took off the cover and saw, smiling up at me, the same dear face that has always given me Christmas greeting first of all, ever since I can remember, I could scarcely contain myself, and it was some time before I cared to dive further into the mysteries of my box.

This is the first Christmas we have ever spent apart, and you have brought yourself as near to me as possible. What a rich girl I am this morning! Not only your own lovely gifts, but tokens from my friends at home, as well. What a good old time you must have had packing them! And the combination letter from all the girls and boys and their dear chaperon! It is a wonder and I have read and re-read it, both to my friends and myself.

I believe the girls are beginning to envy me my Mother. One said the other day: "Miss Taylor, I believe your mother and you are sisters!" Well, I know this, Mother dear: I couldn't have had a sister who would have been my confidential companion as you are. What a mistake some mothers make in holding themselves aloof from their daughters! And how much both mother and daughter miss in such a case!

After hearing other girls talk of having to keep secrets from their mothers for lack of sympathy with their so called silly little pleasures, I know more than ever that my Mother is a gold mine, and value her accordingly.

Now, I come to an important item of news. Irene was singing in my studio the other day, when there was a light rap on the door. I opened it to admit the Herr Prof. who came in, apologizing for the intrusion, but with his countenance beaming. He actually didn't look like a rat at all, and his "Oh, Miss Taylor! What a beautiful, wonderful voice you have! Why did I not know before?" —certainly expressed the gladness he felt.

I hastened to correct him, and when I explained about Irene, and why I was teaching her, he became so enthusiastic, that I thought he would dance. "You have done well, so far," said he, " but would it be intruding if I offer to help? To take her right on from now?" Of course he understands there is no money in it for him, but he exclaimed: "When we hear a voice like this, who thinks of money? We only want to watch and listen to it grow and grow, until it is perfect, as this one is sure to be."

So I have wisely turned my charge over to the Professor's care, but I am to attend the lessons when I wish. Isn't it glorious, Mother, that things do turn out fine sometimes?

Some of the girls are calling me on what they say is important business, so with many thanks for my beautiful Christmas box, and best wishes of the season to my darling Mother—chum, I am

> Your loving daughter
> Virginia

❧

M___ Va., Dec. 28th 19__

My dear girl,

Your Christmas letter in hand, and your lovely gifts. I am more delighted and proud than I can tell you, that you found time in your busy life to make your gifts, for I assure you they are doubly acceptable on that account.

I rejoice with you at the good luck of your friend in enlisting the help of the Professor, and wish her every success.

This must be a note instead of a letter, as we are all going to a dinner party, and Grandfather and the Aunties are waiting for me to get ready. They join me in wishing you a happy New Year, and with a hasty goodbye, I am

> Your loving
> Mother

❧

N.Y. Seminary, Jan. 6th, 19__

My dear Mother,

I must tell you how I spent my holidays, or part of them, at least.

Ella Adams gave a hen-house-party, as she called it. All girls, no men invited. That being the case, six of us were allowed to go, expecially as that

number included a most dignified teacher and chaperon, Miss Virginia Taylor.

Well, we had a great time. Beautiful home and surroundings, carriages,
auto, and above all, the loveliest mother and the jolliest father! They had
planned a week of gayeties for us that fairly took away my breath.

Well we might as well have left our purses behind us, for all the use they
were to us. Mr. Adams is one of the favored of the earth, and he made us
all feel that we were doing him a great favor, every time he opened his pock-
etbook.

Irene was one of our party, and she and I had a room together. I am
getting to be quite fond of her, and wish it would be possible to have her with
us next summer; but that is long way off, and we cannot tell.

Oh, Mother! I am so full of wonderful experiences, that I can scarcely
make my pen go fast enough. One evening Mr. Adams came home with
tickets to a grand concert. The Symphony Orchestra, Señor X, pianist, and
Donald Reid, barytone.

We went, expecting a rare treat, and were not disappointed. The pianist was marvelous, although, as yet, not known in this country: But the
singer took us all by storm. I cannot describe to you how I felt when I heard
him.

His voice was so beautiful, so sympathetic, and his presence was simply
magnetic. I hope I may hear him again. I know I shall never miss an opportunity to do so.

But the strangest thing occurred; we sat in a box at the right of the stage,
facing the first violins, of course, and Irene sat beside me.

A few moments after the orchestra began its first number, she clutched
my arm, and I turned to find her pale as death. I was alarmed, and would
have called for assistance, but she whispered: "It is nothing. The concert-
meister! My Father! Look, but do not call attention!" I did as she requested,
and looking at the first violin beheld— whom do you think? My G string
man! My peeping violinist! No wonder there was trouble in the Roberts
family about music, since the daughter had married that!

I asked no questions, and Irene soon recovered; but after we went to
our room that night, she told me that this man, her father, had persuaded
her mother into a clandestine marriage, and afterwards deserted her, to elope
with an actress of bad reputation.

Her mother died of a broken heart, and Irene was brought up by her grandmother, a widow, whose life was embittered by her daughter's unfortunate marriage and desertion.

Can we blame the old lady for trying to ward off another misfortune, by forbidding her granddaughter music, so as to lessen her opportunity to meet musicians? I suppose she thinks they are all of a kind.

We had a round of theatres, parties, concerts, and an opera before we returned to the seminary, Jan. 2nd, and now we have all settled down to work again.

I know you are having a good time at your old home. Just imagine yourself a girl again, and tell Grandfather for me to watch what beaux you have.

With love to him, and to all the Aunties, and a big Kiss and squeeze for your own dear self, I must say goodbye for this time.

Your daughter,
Virginia

✿

M___, Va., Jan 10th 19__

My dear Virginia,

Your letter found me in the midst of a good old family love-feast, and they all enjoyed it with me. We were so glad of your visit to New York, and laughed at your violinist. I heard some one wonder if you were in danger of losing your heart to the barytone.

I am anxious to know if Irene's father saw her, and recognized her. Why did you leave out that important part?

Mrs. Roberts, no doubt, thinks she is acting wisely in keeping Irene and music apart; but I have always believed it next to impossible to separate a person from a God-given talent. It will find the means of making itself heard.

How did that violinist's picture find a place in your studio? It seems he is not a celebrity, and I cannot understand it.

I shall leave for home in a week, so address your next letter there. This visit will do for me to dream of for a year, when I hope to repeat it. Grandfather says: "Tell Virginia that beaux are as scarce as hens' teeth. My girls are not as they were at a time I well remember, when they had devoted admirers by the score, who carried off every one of them, and left me alone, as far as my home went, but with plenty of doors open to me in theirs."

Grandfather seems so happy to have us all here together, that we hate to break up the family party. Still, Aunt Louise, who has the old home for her own, insists that this reunion shall take place once a year, and we have all agreed. I hope you may be with us next time.

It will do no harm to repeat what I wrote in such a few words, upon receiving my Christmas box from you. The dainty work of your own hands is a source of great pride and pleasure to me. Some people think a musician is good for nothing but music. I say no, and with the contents of this box, I can prove it. Surely it should be natural for fingers to be equally dainty and dextrous with piano and needle!

And now I must stop writing, as there is a clamour for my presence in the sitting-room. They say that I have only a few days more with them, and a whole year to write to Virginia, so, although this letter is shorter than usual, you, I know, will be satisfied to have it so.

Good-bye, dear, and write one about all your little joys and sorrows, as usual, although the latter do not seem to come your way since you have been there, and I am so glad that it is so.

I'm sending you a great package of love, the whole family join with

Your loving Mother

❧

N.Y. Seminary, Jan. 20th 19__

Dear little Mother,

More news, and good news too! But I shall contain myself on this point, until I have answered questions in your letter.

Firstly, no—Irene's father did not recognize her. It seems he was neglectful of his family since she was a little tot, and while she recognized him, both from her own recollection, and from a photo her mother had, (let us hope it was not a duplicate of the one I had), she had outgrown her baby looks, so I suppose her father never knew she was in the audience that night.

I had curiosity enough myself to inquire among the older teachers about the picture in my studio, and find it was put there for a joke on my predecessor, who was very fond of the violin and violinists. Some friend sent her this picture, calling it her ideal.

It was taken down before Irene ever came into the room, and, luckily, I never happened to mention it to her. How badly I should have felt, had I made some of my brilliant remarks in her presence.

Yes, I have had a happy time here, and my separation from you is the only cloud in the sky, so far.

Oh! the best thing has happened, Mother! I must tell you—

One day an elderly lady came to my studio and introduced herself as Mrs. Roberts, saying she was directed there to find her granddaughter. It happened Irene was at that moment in the Herr Prof.'s room, taking a lesson; so I asked her grandmother to wait for her.

Mrs. Roberts said she was glad to have a few moments to become acquainted with me, for it seems Irene had written her about our friendship.

While we talked, that beautiful voice rang out clear and true, and we paused to listen.

"What a wonderful voice!" Mrs. Roberts exclaimed, "Surely that young lady is gifted beyond the ordinary."

I do not know what prompted me, but I asked her if she did not think it would be cruel to keep that girl from reaching a high place in her art. Her answer, I know, will surprise you.

"Indeed it would be cruel. Is there danger of it? If the girl is not financially able I would willingly help in that way myself. I used to have a great notion that music belonged solely to the devil's agents, owing to the bitter experience of one near and dear to me, and even went so far as to forbid Irene ever to know music; although I do not know that she has a particle of talent that way.

"I have changed my views, however, and listening to common sense, I realize that as there is truth in the old saying that one swallow does not make a summer, neither does one unscrupulous, wicked musician, mar the whole world of music."

Oh! how glad I was to tell her that Irene's was the beautiful voice she listened to, and to confess to her my part of the scheme for the girl's education! And later, how we both surprised the happy girl with our plans for her future!

Mrs. Roberts was with us all day, and I quite fell in love with her. She is a charming old lady, and I wouldn't mind having her for a grandmother myself.

Now, for another wonderful experience! It happens that Donald Reid was an old chum and classmate of the Herr Prof. in Germany. It follows that he came here, and the Herr Prof. persuaded him to give a recital for us. It also follows that your humble servant and most unworthy daughter was the accompanist on that occasion. Think of it! It also follows that I have the least little confession to make.

During the evening, what more natural than for the Prof. to call his friend's attention to Irene's voice? Then followed a duet between the two, and, as, I played second fiddle on the piano (figuratively speaking), a sudden thought came to me that e're long, Donald Reid and Irene would be equals in the world of art, while I—oh, well, no matter! But I did have a queer little feeling possess me, that I had never known before. Was it envy, that I had not been given a voice instead of nimble fingers?

A few days later the Herr. Prof. came to me all excitement, with a hurry-up message from his friend. He was to have an important recital, and, at the last minute, almost, his accompanist was suddenly ill. Could Miss Taylor be persuaded to take his place?"

Of course Miss Taylor was only too glad to do so, and together we went to get the necessary permission, which was kindly granted. It was arranged that I should go to Mr. Adams', and Ella was allowed to accompany me, thus settling the matter of propriety.

We had one great rehearsal, and then the recital. Oh, what a success it was! The audience was charmed, and rightly so. Critics were lavish with their praise, even kind to poor little obscure me; as proof of which I send you a clipping from a prominent New York paper, and ask you to read carefully the paragraph which says: "Even though the greatest praise should be bestowed on this young singer, yet the full artistic success of his recital was not due to Donald Reid alone; for the sympathetic, beautiful support given by Miss Virginia Taylor at the piano shows her to be an accompanist of rare talent."

I find in even this short acquaintance with Donald Reid, that the man matches the voice.

I have never met anyone who has so completely taken my fancy. The

Herr. Prof. calls him a Prince among men, and lauds him to the skies, for being able to hold himself aloof from the dissipations and reckless living so often found among men of his profession, flattered as he is.

This kind of friendly devotion, so freely expressed, and Donald Reid's own magnetism, have gone far toward making a blind fool of your little daughter, who comes to you as usual, in confidence, and asks your sympathy in this decidedly one sided romance.

Don't worry, little Mother, girls have been in love before, and the experience didn't kill; so write when you can, and scold if you wish.

Your foolish daughter,
Virginia

A___, Va. Jan 25th 19__

My darling Girlie,

There was much in your letter to answer, and I should touch on all points, did I feel in the mood.

As it is, after telling you of my satisfaction at hearing of Irene's good fortune, and that there is to be no more underhand instruction, I shall take up the subject that seems nearest to you.

I am very much afraid that my little girl has been guilty of giving her heart, unasked. Remember, there is a glamour cast around these artists, that often dazzles foolish girls, and causes them to see a saint or hero where one does not exist.

I do not say it is so in this case, for your professor seems to know so well what manner of man this is.

It is not necessary , though, for me to worry over this, since the romance, as you say, seems to be all on one side.

Above all, Virginia, do not show this infatuation. It would make you ridiculous to outsiders, where your true nature is not known.

To them you would be only one of many foolish maidens, ready to throw yourself at the feet of the man for his art's sake.

To your mother, you are a dear, impulsive girl, taking a short vacation from your sensible self—until this young man goes back to Europe, when *you will have a good laugh at yourself, swear to be an old maid, and a comfort to your old Mother.*

❀

N.Y. Seminary, Jan. 30th 19___

You dear, bad Mother,

You didn't really sympathize with me a bit! I do believe you were laughing at me all the time you wrote that letter. Now, I am going to "get back at you," to use an elegant expression.

This morning there came a letter to me from Donald Reid. At the top was pinned a newspaper notice like the one I sent to you. The note followed, which I copy for your benefit and advice:

"My dear Miss Taylor,

I enclose a clipping which is to your credit, as well as my own, and I fear you may not see it. Hence the liberty I take in addressing you.

Really, this beginning sounds very well indeed, but it is not the real reason for my letter. Short as our acquaintance has been, I know what it has done for me. It is as though I had always known and loved you, and this feeling, perhaps, makes me bolder to say so.

I have a short tour to make before returning to New York. Had hoped to keep this question to myself until I saw you again, but upon deliberation, think it best to give you time—first to wonder at my audacity, and then to forgive me, upon the plea given above.

Is my love altogether hopeless? or, could you care enough for one so unworthy as myself, to think of spending your life with him?

I ask you, in case you do care for me, to inquire, or have your friends inquire about me. My old friend, Herr Schmidt could tell you a little, and put you in the way to satisfy any fears you may have, concerning me.

I want you to know who I am, and what I am, and then, if you can find room in your heart for me, I shall devote my life to your happiness.

You can think of this until my return, next week, when I shall come for my answer. That it may be a favorable one, is the earnest hope and prayer of Donald Reid."

Now, Mother, what shall I do? Here is happiness within my reach, I know it. Perhaps, if I had known him a lifetime, it would not be more proper to accept him than it is now. The only objection is our short acquaintance, and that couldn't be helped, could it, with him in Europe, and me here?

I know you'll say "yes," Mother, for I have had a long talk with Herr Prof. about Donald, and he assures me that any girl may be proud to trust her future to such a man. Why, he even wanted to write to you about him, but I said I believed I could state the case properly and I have.

I await your speedy answer, for I must know what to say when Donald returns, and I know you will not keep me waiting. Remember one thing, Dear Heart, this does not mean separation from you. Where I go, you go, and that shall be in the contract . . .

Your loving,
Virginia

❧

A___, Va., Feb. 2nd 19__

My little Girl,

I have read your letter, and your lover's letter contained therein.

It seems to me a straightforward, manly way of stating things, and I have great faith in your own impressions also.

Taking the recommendations given by your friend, the Professor, I do not see that we can inquire farther.

I have your happiness in view, whatever it may mean to me, and now that the question is up to me, as the slang goes, I shall not stand in the way. Only look to it, you foolish girl, that you bring me as perfect a son-in-law as you have painted. I shall expect a wonderful man, see that I am not disappointed.

Go on in your rosy path, little girl, and may you never have cause to regret the step you are about to take. That your future husband never will, the earnest assertion of

Your devoted
Mother

❧

N.Y. Seminary, Feb. 10th 19__

Mother dear,

Your letter arrived just two days before Donald did, so you see there was need to hurry.

Well, it's all settled for good, and I am the happiest girl in the land.

Now, I shall tell you a huge joke Donald played on me, which he relishes greatly, which I acknowledge, and which you will laugh over first, and then come to the conclusion that you have no earthly objection to Donald Reid for a son-in-law.

Last evening, we were trying some new music, when he turned to me and said: "So you think I can sing, Virginia?" "What a silly question!" I replied. "Do you think I would differ from the world?" "You did not always think so," said he. "You told me once, many years ago, that I had no more voice than a rabbit."

Then everything was clear to me. "You are Mack Smith!" I cried.

"True," he answered. "McDonald Reid Smith at your service. Donald Reid for art's sake, at your suggestion that Mack Smith would not do in that capacity."

"Can't you remember in the old days, when you used to call me Mrs. Smith, because my initials were M.R.S.?" "Now, for your verdict! Are you too angry to forgive?" " No indeed!" I returned. "Only amused and satisfied that I have always known you, and need no recommendation."

Isn't this a for sure romance, little Mother? And just to think Nora knew it all the time, and helped her brother in his barefaced deception! Herr Professor is innocent though, as he never knew Donald by any other name.

We have everything arranged, now. Donald says if he would order a model mother-in-law, he couldn't improve on you, so you're to be a fixture in our home.

After school closes, I'll come back to the dear old place, only to get ready to leave it, as we are to live abroad. When we are well settled over there, Irene is to come to us, and study under the best masters.

Donald goes on quite an extensive tour, starting next week, and I shall *try and get myself settled into common sense enough to do justice to my pupils.*

You didn't think I'd get to study abroad, did you? Well, I'm going to dig hard, when I do get there, to make up for lost time, and you'll see, Mother dear, maybe our hopes may yet be realized.

At any rate, from this time on, this old earth will hold no happier girl than

Your Virginia.

❦

A___, Va., Feb. 16th 19__

My dear Virginia,

Now for your mother's confession!

On bended knees, I humbly beg your pardon for being one in this conspiracy.

Not to marry you off, my dear, never that! But I was in the secret as Donald Reid's identity ever since his sister was here.

She swore me to secrecy, on the plea that her brother wished to surprise his old schoolmate, and see if she would recognize him.

I agreed to keep it from you, although I felt guilty all the time, especially when I saw the way affairs were tending. Did you think for a minute, little girl, that your mother would so readily consent to give you to a perfect stranger? A man she did not know, and had never even seen?

No, indeed! You are too precious to me to let you take such a risk.

I wondered what you thought of my seemingly ready consent. You did not know that I had been schooling myself to this, ever since I received your first gushing letter about the barytone.

That he should love you did not surprise me. I should have wondered at him if he did not.

I always liked Mack (or Donald) when he was a boy, and know by what you have written about him, that he is now even more worthy of my admiration.

So everything is satisfactory to all concerned.

I received a joint letter from Nora and her mother, welcoming me with

you into their family, so there seems to be nothing better to say as an ending to this little romance, than the old time worn sentence:
"They lived in peace."

🌸

This wonderful story was written by Lute Bauer when she was forty-eight, seven years before she accompanied her youngest daughter Katherine to Berlin. I fix the date at 1900 as Lute made a slip of her pen in one of the letters and wrote 1900 instead of 19__. Perhaps in 1900 she was already dreaming of Katherine studying the violin abroad, but was concerned that the family might not be able to afford such a luxury. Though fiction, the story definitely has autobiographical overtones which makes it even dearer to me. I am letting my imagination play but I can't ignore what Lute Bauer appears to have borrowed from her own life experience to include in *A Romance in Fourteen Letters*.

Lute used family names in her story and chose the state of Virginia, interestingly, as the home of the fictional Taylors. Lute's ancestors first lived in Virginia before moving West after the Revolutionary War. Taylor was her mother's family name. The aunties in the story could refer to Lute's real sisters, she had four, one named Mary Louise who died as a child.

Lute Bauer may have studied piano in Europe as her obituary states, and, if so, she may have had a gruff professor and lived in a room two by four feet. But whether she did or not, it is obvious that to study music abroad was an opportunity she considered important for a serious musician at the turn of the century. Lute's heroine in the story, Virginia Taylor, is an accompanist with dreams of being a soloist. We learn quickly that her dream was shared by her mother and that perhaps the death of her father and a financial reversal left the mother and daughter with insufficient funds for European study. They conclude God had other plans for Virginia Taylor. My guess is that Lute Bauer may too have dreamed of being a concert pianist but was denied that opportunity for some reason, probably financial. Maybe Lute taught piano before marrying George Bauer and came to accept her role as wife, mother, accompanist as sufficiently fulfilling. We know Lute Bauer was an accomplished seamtress as well as pianist. Like Virginia Taylor she had nimble fingers.

Lute Bauer was reported to be "fun" and her writings certainly suggest her sense of humor. I think she was writing of her own philosophy of life when she talked in the story of her tendency to see the ridiculous in life, and that as a child she had taken as her life creed: "A merry heart doeth good like a medicine, but a broken spirit dryeth the bones."

I believe Lucy B. B. Bauer lived her motto and in so doing touched and cheered the lives of family and friends.

The Ancestry of Lucy Bushrod Branham Bauer
The Branham and Taylor Families

As a child I was told that my name, Beverly, was a family name, a name which my paternal grandmother had suggested to my parents. Though I always thought Beverly a rather long name to add to Raffensperger, I liked the idea that it was a family name. Not until I untangled the ancestry of my great-grandmother Lucy B. B. Bauer did I discover the source of my name. There were several Beverlys in her ancestry, the first being the daughter of a Henry Beverly.

The family of my great-grandmother, Babboo's mother, was an interesting one. Her heritage was primarily English, though one early ancestor appears to have been Norman and another to have descended from German nobility. The Branham name is English and alludes to "high pastures."

The eldest daughter of Edward and Frances Taylor Branham, Lucy Bushrod Branham could trace her Branham ancestry back to the Vawters and the Ruckers, both families emigrating from England in the mid to late 1600s. Settling in Virginia the families intermarried and served their new country in the military. Lucy Branham's great-grandfather, Achilles Stapp, who had married a Margaret Vawter, fought in the American Revolution. Born in 1755 in Culpepper County, Virginia, Stapp served in the Virginia State Line as a private under Captain Joseph Spencer in the 7th Virginia Regiment commanded by Colonel Alexander McClenaham. It is thought that Achilles Stapp fought at the Battle of Trenton before his discharge from the Army in 1778. Following the Revolutionary War, the Stapps and Vawters moved West settling in Scott County, Kentucky.

Achilles and Margaret Stapp's daughter, Nancy, married Robert Branham born in Culpepper, Virginia, in 1787. His father, John Branham had served as corporal in the Virginia Continental Line. John

The Branhams & Taylors

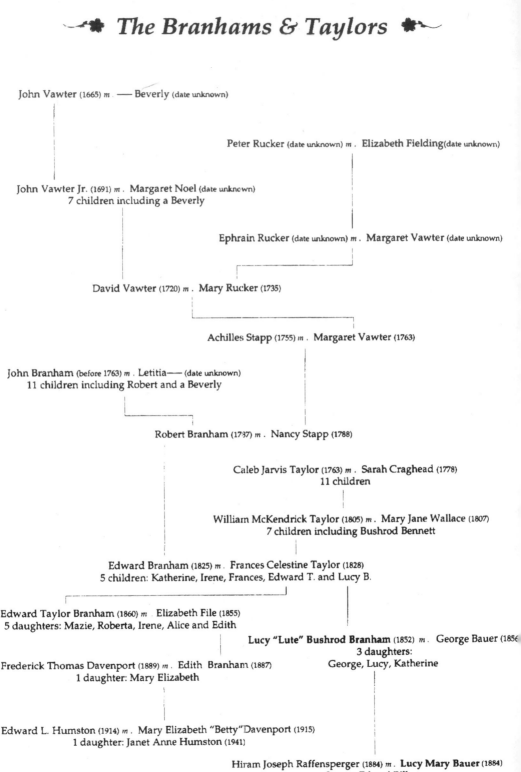

John Vawter (1665) *m* . —— Beverly (date unknown)

Peter Rucker (date unknown) *m* . Elizabeth Fielding (date unknown)

John Vawter Jr. (1691) *m* . Margaret Noel (date unknown)
7 children including a Beverly

Ephrain Rucker (date unknown) *m* . Margaret Vawter (date unknown)

David Vawter (1720) *m* . Mary Rucker (1735)

Achilles Stapp (1755) *m* . Margaret Vawter (1763)

John Branham (before 1763) *m* . Letitia—— (date unknown)
11 children including Robert and a Beverly

Robert Branham (1737) *m* . Nancy Stapp (1788)

Caleb Jarvis Taylor (1763) *m* . Sarah Craghead (1778)
11 children

William McKendrick Taylor (1805) *m* . Mary Jane Wallace (1807)
7 children including Bushrod Bennett

Edward Branham (1825) *m* . Frances Celestine Taylor (1828)
5 children: Katherine, Irene, Frances, Edward T. and Lucy B.

Edward Taylor Branham (1860) *m* . Elizabeth File (1855)
5 daughters: Mazie, Roberta, Irene, Alice and Edith

Lucy "Lute" Bushrod Branham (1852) *m* . George Bauer (1856
3 daughters:
George, Lucy, Katherine

Frederick Thomas Davenport (1889) *m* . Edith Branham (1887)
1 daughter: Mary Elizabeth

Edward L. Humston (1914) *m* . Mary Elizabeth "Betty" Davenport (1915)
1 daughter: Janet Anne Humston (1941)

Hiram Joseph Raffensperger (1884) *m* . Lucy Mary Bauer (1884)
2 sons: Ed and Bill

and his wife Letitia moved their family West to Kentucky following the American Revolution. Robert and Nancy Stapp Branham had one son, Edward, born in 1825, after moving across the Ohio River to North Madison, Indiana.

Edward Branham became a wholesale shoe merchant and married Frances Celestine Taylor, daughter of Judge William McKendrick Taylor of Madison and Mary Jane Wallace born in Hamilton County, Ohio in 1807. The Taylor Family Bible, which I inherited, is a large leather-bound Bible published in Philadelphia in 1805. The Taylor family used this Bible to record their family history beginning with the Reverend Caleb Jarvis Taylor, who was born in 1763 in St. Mary's County, Maryland. In 1791 he married a Sarah Craghead of Pennsylvania and they moved west to Campbell County, Kentucky. Between 1792 and 1815 Caleb and Sarah Taylor had eleven children, all born in either Mayson or Campbell Counties.

Reverend Caleb Jarvis Taylor was one of the early Methodist preachers in Kentucky. According to a news article Reverend Taylor "possessed considerable poetic ability and wrote many of the songs sung by the people of Kentucky." His son, William McKendrick, however, chose to study law. William left his childhood home with a bundle of clothes and a New Testament given to him by Bishop William McKendrick, for whom he was named. In a news article Judge William McKendrick Taylor was quoted as saying, "When the moment came for me to leave my kind and affectionate mother, she informed me she wished to make one last request of me: 'I want you to promise me to pray to God three times every day you are gone and then I shall cheerfully resign my poor orphan boy from my sight, knowing that God will take care of you.' On this single promise I have built all the character of life I have up to the present day." William Taylor and his wife Mary Jane had eight children born in Madison, Indiana, all with most interesting given names: Cerene Applia, Bushrod Bennett, Margaret Strange, Mary Jane, Sarah Hamline, William McKendrick, Jr., Eliza Donna Brook, and Frances Celestine, Lute Bauer's mother.

Frances Taylor and Edward Branham had five daughters and two sons in Madison, Indiana, before moving their family to Indianapolis in 1863. Their daughters were Lucy Bushrod (Lute), Katherine Vir-

Edward and Frances Taylor Branham. Both born in Madison, they moved their family to Indianapolis.

The Branham children—(from left) Kate, Rene, Fan, Edward T., and Lute.

ginia (Kate), Cerene (Rene), Mary Louise, and Frances Celestine (Fan)—named after her mother. Firstborn Lucy received her middle name from an uncle, Frances' brother Bushrod Bennett Taylor, also of Madison. Bushrod Taylor's home is shown in the book *The Early Architecture of Madison, Indiana.* Now known as the Wilbur-Reindollar house, it was originally a one-and-a-half-story brick farmhouse with a southern influence. Located at 226 Maywood Lane the house has several outbuildings and views of the Ohio River. It was built in the early 1830s by Shadrack Wilbur. Bushrod Taylor was the third owner.

Katherine Virginia Branham, called Kate, never married. She became a librarian and eventually served with distinction as the head of the Reference Library of the central Indianapolis Public Library. On Kate's retirement she received a citation from the mayor of a "grateful city." Rene married Edward Briggs; they had no children. Mary Louise died at age twelve of "spinal fever" according to a death notice pasted in the Taylor Family Bible. Fan, the beauty of the Branham girls, married Lyle Clough. They adopted a daughter, Margaret, who married Philip Johnson. Their son was named Philip as well.

The eldest son of Edward and Frances Taylor Branham was Robert, born in 1856. He died at the age of one in Madison, Indiana. The surviving son, Edward Taylor, was born in 1860 in Madison, moving with his family to Indianapolis at the age of four. Edward graduated from the old Indianapolis High School (which became Shortridge) in 1877. He married Mary Elizabeth File, a teacher of English at the Indianapolis School for the Blind in 1883. As a young man, Lute Bauer's only brother was a traveling shoe salesman for their father's company, McKee & Branham Wholesale House. Later in life he became president of the Indianapolis Wire Bound Box Company and was prominent in various civic organizations. A devout Christian and Sunday School teacher, he was nicknamed "Belzie" by family members. Belzie was short for Beelzebub (Satan), the antithesis of his personality and faith. Edward Taylor Branham first joined the Edwin Ray Methodist Episcopal Church, later becoming an active member of the Irvington Methodist Church and the Irvington Masonic Lodge on the east side of Indianapolis.

Lucy Bushrod Branham Bauer (L.B.B.B.) was Aunt Lute to the five daughters of her younger brother Edward: Mazie, Roberta, Irene, Alice, and Edith. Mazie Branham married and became Mrs. William Iuppenlatz of Indianapolis. Roberta and Irene didn't marry; Roberta remained in Indianapolis while Irene moved to Bakersfield, California. Alice Branham married H. T. Bradley and moved to Houston and then to St. Louis, Missouri. Alice Bradley traced the family genealogy with the assistance of her aunt Kate Branham. Edith Branham married Frederick Thomas Davenport called "Ted." When I was in elementary school, my grandparents Raffensperger took me along when they visited Edith and Ted Davenport at their home by Fall Creek in Indianapolis. The Davenports were warm and friendly people. I was fascinated with their playhouse, which was built on "stilts" as the area often flooded. Their daughter Betty Davenport Humston and granddaughter Janet Anne Humston shared with me their memories and photographs of the Branhams, Bauers, and Raffenspergers.